CAROLINE SAUNDERS

BETTER
THAN
LIFE

HOW TO STUDY THE BIBLE
AND <u>LIKE</u> IT

Lifeway PRESS®
NASHVILLE, TENNESSEE

W9-BQV-806

EDITORIAL TEAM

BEN TRUEBLOOD
Director, Student Ministry

JOHN PAUL BASHAM
*Manager, Student
Ministry Publishing*

KAREN DANIEL
Editorial Team Leader

MORGAN HAWK
Content Editor

JENNIFER SIAO
Production Editor

SARAH SPERRY
Graphic Designer

Published by LifeWay Press® // © 2020 Caroline Saunders

ISBN: 9781087701561 // Item Number: 005823978

Dewey Decimal Classification Number: 242.2
Subject Heading: DEVOTIONAL LITERATURE /
BIBLE STUDY AND TEACHING / GOD

Printed in the United States of America

Student Ministry Publishing // LifeWay Resources
One LifeWay Plaza // Nashville, TN 37234-0144

We believe that the Bible has God for its author; salvation for its end; and truth, without any mixture of error, for its matter and that all Scripture is totally true and trustworthy. To review LifeWay's doctrinal guideline, please visit www.lifeway.com/doctrinalguideline.

CONTENTS

ABOUT THE AUTHOR

CAROLINE SAUNDERS is a writer, pastor's wife, and mother of three who believes in taking Jesus seriously and being un-serious about nearly everything else. She loves serving women through writing, through her church, and through a parachurch women's ministry she started with her best friends (StoryandSoulWeekend.com). Find her writing, resources, and ridiculousness at WriterCaroline.com and on Instagram @writercaroline.

HOW TO USE

This (very cute) book contains nine weeks of group sessions, eight weeks of personal study wedged between them, and a leader guide. You'll start each week with your group, learning together through video teaching and group discussion. It's my prayer that the group sessions will spur you on to connect with God's Word and with one another in an energizing, meaningful way! Then, on your own, you'll complete four days of personal study before coming together again for the next week's group session. I hope that you'll flex your spiritual muscles as best you can to faithfully complete the personal study days! They're designed to be engaging, interesting, and informative, and I think you'll discover that learning to study God's Word over the next nine weeks is a solid investment of your time. Here's a breakdown of the elements of the study:

BIBLE STUDY BOOK

In addition to the confetti on the cover (a very important element), this book features:

Group Discussion

Video listening guides and group discussion questions are provided to help your group engage with each week's content.

Personal Study

Four days of personal Bible study each week will help the group discussion content soak into your heart and will expose you to new layers of learning. I'll also share weird and funny tidbits and stories, because I like to pretend we're hanging out each day.

Leader Guide

In the back of the book, we placed a leader guide to help support leaders as they support you. (Hi leaders! We love you!)

THE FLOW

Design your group sessions to fit the space, time, and needs of your girls.

Learn with Your Group

Launch each week with a group session. You can begin the session with a short icebreaker and then settle in for the teaching video. As you listen, use the Watch guide to help you stay on track and to give you that satisfying "fill-in-the-blank" feeling. When the teaching video is done, use the discussion guide to talk about what you've learned and to dig in deeper.

Learn on Your Own

Ideally, you'll leave your group session energized to continue learning! If you don't, you can use your spiritual muscles to press on anyway, knowing that delight lives on the other side of discipline. Keep an eye out for opportunities God's given you to study His Word. Sometimes we don't think we have the time because we aren't watching for it!

HEY, GIRL.

I might as well begin this study with a confession: When I graduated from college and found myself responsible for my own dinner (Ugh!), I tried to cook based on instinct. This went great! (No, it didn't.) My husband still remembers something I made called "Biscuit Chicken Cheese Casserole," which isn't a creative name at all, just a list of the literal ingredients. I plopped chicken, cheese, and a can of biscuits in a pan, cooked it at 350 degrees, and acted like I was a genius. Yikes! My husband said, "Please stop inventing food and maybe try to follow a recipe." I responded, "Recipes are oppressive! I am a free woman!" He loves me.

I resisted recipes because they seemed so bossy. (Don't tell me to use a half teaspoon of salt! I do what I want!) But do you know what crucial piece of information I was missing? I didn't realize the structure of a recipe is what supports a dinner's potential for deliciousness and delight. I thought I was choosing the more fun path by opting for less structure, but I was actually setting myself up for less fun.

A few years after this light bulb kitchen moment, I realized the same concept applied to Bible reading. You see, I'd been coming to the Bible for years with no recipe, reading whatever I felt like reading so I could check the box and feel like a good Christian girl. Even with the bit of structure a reading plan provides, I wasn't gobbling up the words like a delicious piece of cake but was hazily watching them go by, like an uninteresting Netflix binge. The result wasn't delight but drudgery.

Armed with this new realization, I began to seek information wherever I could, and I soon found that reading the Bible in a meaningful, transformative way involves more than just watching the words go by. There are tools we can use and recipes we can employ to really sink our teeth into what God is saying. When I learned how to study the Bible, I found that I truly liked to study the Bible. Once again, structure led to delight, and I have not been the same since.

My people will tell you I love my Bible with my whole heart, and I want to help you love the Bible with your whole heart, too. I want you to know "it is no empty word for you, but your very life" (Deut. 32:47) because it tells you what God is like and that will compel you to worship and give Him everything you have. That's the heart behind this study, which functions kind of like an interactive recipe book. Everything centers on a basic recipe constructed from methods and tools Bible lovers have employed in one way or another for a long time in their pursuit to know and love God. This recipe is COIA, or, more specifically C (5Ws + H) + O (DTR) + I (SGC) + A. Confused yet? Don't worry, sister, I'm going to walk you through it bit by bit like a quirky cooking show, and by the end of it, I think you'll know how to study the Bible and like it.

I am so excited for you to "taste and see that the LORD is good" (Ps. 34:8) and genuinely proclaim, "How sweet are your words to my taste, sweeter than honey to my mouth!" (Ps. 119:103).

Forks up!

COIA METHOD

CONTEXT WHAT WAS GOING ON IN THE WORLD WHEN THIS WAS WRITTEN?

5 Ws & H WHO WHAT WHEN WHERE WHY HOW

OBSERVATION WHAT DOES IT SAY?

DTR DEFINITIONS THEMES REPETITION

INTERPRETATION WHAT DOES IT MEAN?

SGC SCRIPTURE GOSPEL CURIOSITY

APPLICATION HOW DOES THIS CHANGE THE WAY I THINK AND LIVE?

PSALM 63

1 *O God, you are my God; earnestly I seek you;*

my soul thirsts for you;

my flesh faints for you,

as in a dry and weary land where there is no water.

2 *So I have looked upon you in the sanctuary,*

beholding your power and glory.

3 *Because your steadfast love is better than life,*

my lips will praise you.

4 *So I will bless you as long as I live;*

in your name I will lift up my hands.

5 *My soul will be satisfied as with fat and rich food,*

and my mouth will praise you with joyful lips,

6 *when I remember you upon my bed,*

and meditate on you in the watches of the night;

7 for you have been my help,

and in the shadow of your wings I will sing for joy.

8 My soul clings to you;

your right hand upholds me.

9 But those who seek to destroy my life

shall go down into the depths of the earth;

10 they shall be given over to the power of the sword;

they shall be a portion for jackals.

11 But the king shall rejoice in God;

all who swear by him shall exult,

for the mouths of liars will be stopped.

Use this copy of Psalm 63 to take notes for the entirety of the study. Mark it up and make it your own!

THE RECIPE: COIA

SESSION ONE

PSALM 63

1 *O God, you are my God; earnestly I seek you;*

my soul thirsts for you;

my flesh faints for you,

as in a dry and weary land where there is no water.

2 *So I have looked upon you in the sanctuary,*

beholding your power and glory.

3 *Because your steadfast love is better than life,*

my lips will praise you.

4 *So I will bless you as long as I live;*

in your name I will lift up my hands.

5 *My soul will be satisfied as with fat and rich food, and my mouth*

will praise you with joyful lips,

6 *when I remember you upon my bed,*

and meditate on you in the watches of the night;

7 *for you have been my help,*

and in the shadow of your wings I will sing for joy.

8 *My soul clings to you;*

your right hand upholds me.

9 *But those who seek to destroy my life*

shall go down into the depths of the earth;

10 *they shall be given over to the power of the sword;*

they shall be a portion for jackals.

11 *But the king shall rejoice in God;*

all who swear by him shall exult,

for the mouths of liars will be stopped.

WATCH

Watch the video and fill in the blanks before transitioning to the Discuss section.

The point of Bible reading is not to kindle God's affection for ___us___. It's to kindle our affection for ___him___.

Delight must be propped up by ___structure___.

The Recipe: COIA

C - ___context___

O - ___observation___

I - ___interpretation___

A - ___application___

CONTEXT: 5Ws and H

___who___, ___what___, ___when___, ___where___, ___why___, and ___how___.

OBSERVATION: What does this ___say___?

The goal is ___comprehension___.

INTERPRETATION: What does it ___mean___?

APPLICATION: How does this change the way I think and feel?

There are two marks of being a follower of Christ:

1. obedience | sanctification

2. justification

DISCUSS

What's something that delights you? (Think "normal person delight," not "spiritual delight.") What's something that's easy for you to do because you like it?

READ PSALM 119:97,103,127.

How does the psalmist feel about God's Word?

Take a few minutes for private reflection and consider honestly: What's your relationship like with God's Word? Do you understand how to read it in a meaningful way? Do you enjoy it? Journal your thoughts. Afterward, share your reflections about your relationship with God's Word with your group.

> I have always struggled getting into God's word. I manage to pray every day but I don't feel like there is a strong relationship. It always feels like a chore so I hope this book helps.

(**And psst — there's no shame here! God has searched you and knows you (Ps. 139:1), so He has already discerned your honest position here. You are safe to be honest!**)

List some reasons you've heard stating why we should study the Bible.
- get closer to God
- being a "good christian"

Why do you think we should study the Bible? How did the video help your understanding of this question?

When it comes to Bible reading, whose delight needs work? God's delight in us, or our delight in Him? Explain.

> Our delight in him. Our relationship w/ God is not for his pleasure, it's for ours.

13 | THE RECIPE: COIA

"And may you have the power to understand, as all God's people should, how wide, how long, how high, and how deep his love is. May you experience the love of Christ, though it is too great to understand fully. Then you will be made complete with all the fullness of life and power that comes from God" **(NLT)**

How might this prayer be a helpful one for us to borrow as we seek to learn how to study the Bible and like it?

> It talks about diving into his word and why we should.

If you read the intro to this study, you know all about "Biscuit Chicken Cheese" casserole, an unfortunate result of my refusal to be bossed around by recipes. I followed my instincts rather than structure, and let's just say, it didn't do my taste buds any favors.

It can feel backward for a serious thing like structure to be the catalyst for something unserious, like delight, but that's exactly how God designed the world to work. The structure of a recipe is what supports a dinner's potential for deliciousness and delight.

Can you think of something delightful that requires structure?

Have you ever tried to cook without a recipe? How did it go?

> I don't think I've ever cooked w/out a recipe AT ALL but I'm not good at improvising in the kitchen.

Recipes, though they can seem a little bossy at the onset, are actually a wonderful foundation for yummy stuff. This extends beyond food into all kinds of things, particularly Bible reading. When we read the Bible without a recipe, we can wind up with the spiritual equivalent of Biscuit Chicken Cheese Casserole, and though I don't think it will kill you, it may keep you from truly delighting in God's Word.

Do you remember the Bible reading recipe we learned today? Write it here:

Delight is always propped up by STRUCTURE

LET'S TALK ABOUT EACH ELEMENT

CONTEXT

Why does context matter in Bible reading?

Has something you've said ever been repeated to another person out of context? How did you respond?

OBSERVATION

What's the main goal of observation?

Observation seems simple, but we often skip over it. Why do you think that is?

INTERPRETATION

What's the main goal of interpretation?

Have you ever received a confusing text and spent time wondering, "What does it mean?"

Have your words ever been misinterpreted? What did you do in response?

APPLICATION

What is the main goal of application?

Do you ever notice yourself rushing to application when you read the Bible? Why is it important that this is the last part of the recipe and not the first?

READ EPHESIANS 2:8-10.

How do these verses help us navigate that justification/sanctification stuff?

Hint: "not a result of works" in verse 9 and "created in Christ Jesus for good works" in verse 10.

READ JAMES 1:22.

Why does application matter?

Based on what you know about the difference between justification—Jesus exchanging our guilt for His righteousness—and sanctification—God's active, daily work in moving us to be more like Christ—what's a good way to apply James 1:22 to daily living?

CLOSING PRAYER

DEAR GOD,

You are our God. We want to earnestly seek You. Thank You that we can seek You through Your words in the Bible.

AMEN.

CLOSING RHYTHM

Read the entire passage aloud together. (I KNOW THIS IS WEIRD. Just be weird.)

DAY 1: CONTEXT

When I choose a book or a passage to study, I like to spend the first day researching context because it sets a great foundation for the rest of the Bible reading process. There are several things you can do to research context, but I like to look in the text itself first. So, let's do that.

Scan Psalm 63. Do you see any clues that help you understand the context? Use the space below to start collecting context information on the 5Ws and H. Don't feel like you have to find everything, and feel free to be as messy as you like on this page. (We'll use the Context Chart on page 28 next week when we deep-dive into context, and you may end up copying a few answers over.) As you search, here's a pro-tip: don't forget the italicized information just below the psalm's title. This is called the superscription, and often the superscription can provide helpful context.

WHO

Who wrote it and to whom are they writing?

WHAT

What was the world like when it was written (cultural norms, big events, and so on)?

WHEN

When did they write it?

WHERE

Where was the author when he wrote it? Consider more than just his literal location—perhaps his position in the culture.

WHY

Why was it written? What was the purpose for writing it?

HOW

How was it written? What genre did the author write it in?

Based on the 5Ws, take a moment to think: Would you read a note from a teacher differently than you'd read a note from your best friend? Would you read a note from a person in prison differently than you'd read a note from a person at Disney World? Would you read a note differently if it was written to someone else versus written specifically to you? Why is it important for us to pay attention to the author, the author's circumstances, the audience, and the audience's circumstances when we read?

This superscription says, "A psalm of David." Most of us have never looked up the word "psalm" because for anyone who has been in church for a while, the word probably seems commonplace. But use an online dictionary like Merriam-Webster to look up this word. Let the definition inform your answer for H.

> Why is it important for us, as Christians, to pay attention to when something is a poem or song versus when something is law, like the Ten Commandments?

CLOSING PRAYER

DEAR GOD,

You are our God. We want to earnestly seek You. Thank You that we can seek You through Your words in the Bible. Give us wisdom today as we learn from what David wrote about You thousands of years ago.

AMEN.

CLOSING RHYTHM

Consider David's physical location—a wilderness. Reread Psalm 63 (out loud if you can), and try to understand what it would be like to pen these words in a literal wilderness.

DAY 2: OBSERVATION

Do you ever open your Bible and think, "Okay, it's time to be transformed! Time to be a better human! Time to morph into a super spiritual person! Time to check this off my list so I can avoid guilt! Time to learn a nugget of truth so I won't have a terrible day!"

If you have any of these thoughts when you open your Bible, you're not alone. These are all really normal thoughts.

Take a moment and consider the thoughts you generally have when you open your Bible. Write them below.

Okay, now mentally wad those thoughts up into a ball and toss them in the trash can. For some reason, Bible reading can seem more intense than normal reading. In a way, this demonstrates our conviction that the Bible is special, but it can also get squirrelly and prevent us from effectively interacting with the Bible. As I've learned from one of my favorite Bible teachers, Jen Wilkin, the Bible is certainly more than a book, but it's at least a book.[1] I love this thought, because it feels like an invitation to settle down a bit.

For today, I want us to keep all the weird thoughts in the trash, settle down, and simply read a passage of the Bible like we'd read any other passage of writing. Observation means paying attention to the text and asking, "What does this say?"

Read Psalm 63 (out loud, if possible) and make five observations. Don't overthink it—just find things you observe that the text says, such as David is satisfied by the Lord (v. 5).

1.

2.

3.

4.

5.

Guess what? That's it! We'll talk more about observation as we dig deeper into Psalm 63, but for now, remember this: Observation means paying attention to the text and asking, "What does it say?"

CLOSING PRAYER

DEAR GOD,

You are my God. I want to earnestly seek You. Thank You that I can seek You through Your words in the Bible. When I open my Bible, open my eyes and sharpen my mind so that I can pay close attention to Your words and know You better.

AMEN.

DAY 3: INTERPRETATION

I was once making blueberry muffins, and the recipe said, "Fold the blueberries into the batter." I don't know about you, but I don't know how to fold food unless it's a taco or something. Blueberries and batter are inherently not foldable, and this conundrum made me want to scream. How does one fold non-foldable food? The question I yelled at the cookbook was, "WHAT DOES THIS MEAN?" (Are you guys getting concerned about me in the kitchen? Prayers up.)

Once again, I was the victim of misinterpretation. I interpreted "fold" to mean the same thing it means when I'm faced with a giant heap of laundry. But in the kitchen, "fold" means "to incorporate (a food ingredient) into a mixture by repeated gentle overturnings without stirring or beating."[2] (Side-note: See how context is everything? How "fold" means one thing in the laundry room and another thing in the kitchen?)

Here's the point: The interpretation part of the recipe is where things can get a little tricky. It's like detective work. You have to get out a magnifying glass and examine the footprints, searching each one for clues, like "What does this mean?"

Bible interpretation is even stickier than recipe interpretation, because while the distance between a "kitchen fold" and a "laundry room fold" is significant, at least the two rooms share a house and a culture and a language. But the Bible was originally written in a different language than ours by a writer with a different culture than ours to an audience with a different culture than ours. You can see how that might complicate things.

Here's the thing: I've been explaining the COIA recipe as if it's really simple, but simple doesn't necessarily mean easy. Scripture often requires some heavy lifting. You will feel the discomfort that a detective must feel before she cracks the case, and you might even feel dumb sometimes, like I did when I thought the cookbook asked me to fold food like laundry. The discomfort and the dumb feeling—those are totally normal. However, in those moments, we get to remember the good news of the gospel—Jesus bore our shame on the cross! God's affection for us is not wrapped up in how quickly we can understand the Bible. Through the encouragement of the gospel, we get to decide to persevere through the tough stuff.

Close your eyes and picture yourself wearing one of those weird British detective hats like Sherlock Holmes. You are a detective now, except, thank goodness, this is an invisible hat and will not cause you any deep embarrassment.

Now, while you're wearing your imaginary, terrible hat, read Psalm 63 like you'd scan a crime scene and collect evidence. Put a tiny question mark above any place in the text that looks like it needs further investigating. What fingerprints and footprints do you see?

Jot some notes below of the places that intrigue or confuse you:

What verse are you most looking forward to investigating further?

What verse makes you go "HUH?"

You know what? The Bible is hard. God made it that way so we'd lean in close to Him and ask, "What did You mean by that?" He is so awesome that way. We'll take a closer look at every part of this passage in the weeks to come, but for now, you can take off your invisible and unfashionable detective hat. You did it! How do you feel? Confused? Overwhelmed? Itchy because the fake hat is made of wool?

CLOSING PRAYER

DEAR GOD,

You are my God. I want to earnestly seek You. Thank You that I can seek You through Your words in the Bible. Thank You for making everything a little mysterious so that I have to depend on You. I want to know You more!

AMEN.

CLOSING RHYTHM

Read the entire passage aloud, or listen to the Psalm 63 song you found yesterday. (If you didn't have chance, check out some of my favorites listed in the back.) Either way, this repetition is a great way to get the text deep into your bones.

DAY 4: APPLICATION

Congrats! You've gotten to the very last part of the recipe, and we have set approximately zero fires in the proverbial kitchen. The end of the recipe is A, and A is for Application. That means we come to it and ask, "How should this change the way I think or live?"

Because we live in a world addicted to New Year's Resolutions, self-help books, and social media accounts so shiny they hurt our eyes and wither our souls, I want to always remind you of the gospel when we get to the application part of the recipe. Remember: God is more concerned with our true nearness to Him than with our outward appearance of nearness to Him. He is a good parent, who is always going to simultaneously invite you deeper into relationship as He invites you into deeper obedience. Think about this:

What would it be like to have a parent-child relationship that requires obedience but does not invite relationship?

What would it be like to have a parent-child relationship that invites relationship but does not require obedience?

Darling girl, you are loved by the God of the universe who, unbelievably, offers us a sacred thing: membership into His family. Family is just about the most precious thing that God created, and that's what He extends to you through Jesus!

Here's how I like to think of it: God is so all-knowing that it's as if our entire souls have been scanned like a carry-on bag at the airport. He's seen every nook and cranny of our souls, every sin, every desire, every yucky thing about us that even we aren't aware of. He knew we could never make our way to Him on our own—our sin was too heavy. So He came to us. He took on flesh and entered the world the same way we did: as a baby. He endured trials and temptations but responded differently than we did: sinlessly. Then He took our sin and shame and died like a criminal on our behalf. We were the true criminals. But when Jesus died on the cross, this sacrifice was sufficient payment for our criminality—every big and small sin hiding in the crevices of our souls, spewing from our mouths, lurking in our hearts. But Jesus' death did more than pay for the sins—it was also an invitation from the Lord: Be my daughter.

Do you see? We obey not because God is a meanie who likes to control us. We obey because He is our good Father who spared nothing to save us, who knows we are criminals in our hearts, but insists upon offering us a seat at His table. Can you believe it? Is there anyone else like Him? No!

As you consider what change a passage should bring about in your life, always remember this gospel story. Otherwise, you are at risk of reading Scripture and thinking you can save yourself by hustling and making yourself into God's image using your own strength. That's not how this works. We read God's Word and humbly ask, "God, how do You want this to change me?" And we let God have access to whatever He wants. We work in partnership with Him by surrendering our wants for His will, day by day, in millions of tiny choices. Then we look in the mirror one wonderful day and we think with joy, "Hey, I'm more like Jesus than I was."

For today, let's do a small but mighty bit of application. Read the first part of verse one, and fill in the missing words below:

"O God, you are _____ God."

The first several times I read this passage, I overlooked this small word. But thanks to the "O" part of the recipe, I remembered to slow down and pay attention. When I noticed the "my," my brain immediately went into the second part of the recipe "I" and thought, "Wow! That is such an intimate phrasing. Why did David start his psalm this way?"

We'll wrestle with that more in the days to come, but for now, I want you to remember the gospel story and ask yourself a crucial application question:

Is God your God? Do you relate to this personal relationship that David clearly has with God?

Take some time to process your relationship with God, and share a bit about it in the space below.

CLOSING PRAYER

Write your own closing prayer today. Feel free to borrow language from Psalm 63 if you can't find the words.

DEAR GOD,

_____

_____

_____

_____

_____

_____

_____

_____

_____

_____

_____

_____

_____

_____

_____

AMEN.

CLOSING RHYTHM

Read the entire passage aloud, or listen to the Psalm 63 song you found earlier this week. Either way, this repetition is a great way to get the text deep into your bones.

If you didn't have a chance, check out some of my favorites at the back of the book.

CONTEXT MATTERS

SESSION TWO

PSALM 63

1 *O God, you are my God; earnestly I seek you;*

my soul thirsts for you;

my flesh faints for you,

as in a dry and weary land where there is no water.

2 *So I have looked upon you in the sanctuary,*

beholding your power and glory.

3 *Because your steadfast love is better than life,*

my lips will praise you.

4 *So I will bless you as long as I live;*

in your name I will lift up my hands.

5 *My soul will be satisfied as with fat and rich food, and my mouth*

will praise you with joyful lips,

6 *when I remember you upon my bed,*

and meditate on you in the watches of the night;

7 *for you have been my help,*

and in the shadow of your wings I will sing for joy.

8 *My soul clings to you;*

your right hand upholds me.

9 *But those who seek to destroy my life*

shall go down into the depths of the earth;

10 *they shall be given over to the power of the sword;*

they shall be a portion for jackals.

11 *But the king shall rejoice in God;*

all who swear by him shall exult,

for the mouths of liars will be stopped.

WATCH

Watch the video and fill in the blanks before transitioning to the Discuss section.

"I guess you had to be there" is a way of saying "_____ _____."

This text is not designed to give you rules to _____ but to show you the God you can _____.

His (David's) _____ has some very serious _____.

CONTEXT CHART

You can add all of your notes below from the video and your group discussion time.

W WHO

W WHAT

W WHEN

W WHERE

W WHY

H HOW

DISCUSS

Have you ever tried to retell a story of something funny that happened, and despite how hard you and others laughed at the time, the people hearing the story just didn't understand why it was so funny?

Why is it important to have context?

Have you ever thought about considering the context when you're reading the Bible? Why or why not?

Is there anything we already know about King David? Add it to your context chart if it's not already there.

Do you remember the Bible reading recipe we're using? Have each person in the group say it. We're primarily focusing on the "C" part of the recipe, context, but keep an eye out for all the elements of the recipe in today's discussion.

Read Psalm 63 together with the *context* in mind, try to *observe* ("what does it say?") the text, and then discuss what you find. Specifically keep an eye out for two things:

1. Relationship things—anything that gives clues about David's relationship with God and with others. I underlined these things in pink, but you can do whatever makes sense to you.

2. Setting things—anything that gives clues about David's physical context. I marked these things with a yellow highlighter, but you can do whatever makes sense to you.

With your group, *interpret* the text. Specifically, "What does it mean?"

1. Considering the extreme ways David broke God's laws in his past and the difficult position he's in right now, what is the significance of the words "you" and "my" in the first part of verse 1? Circle "you" and "my" in the text because we'll continue to think on it.

2. David doesn't have a great track record when it comes to sin, and we know that sin keeps us from being close with the Lord. And yet, despite all he's done, David is still bold enough to say, "You are my God." Why is that? What's the thing that allows him to be close to the Lord despite all he's done?

O God,
you are
my God!

3. Compare verse 1 with verse 9. What relationship is revealed in each verse? Why do you think David displays such different postures in these two relationships?

With your group, *apply* the text. Specifically, answer:

1. Despite all David has done, he's still bold enough to say, "You are my God" because God is a God who forgives grievous[1] sin and allows sinners to be in an intimate relationship with Him. Do you believe this about God? How does the truth about His character impact you?

2. Read verse 1. David is literally in a "dry and weary land," but the thirst he talks about is more than a physical thirst—it's a spiritual thirst. Have you ever been spiritually thirsty?

3. Have you ever encountered a spiritually "dry and weary land"? Explain.

With your group, complete the context chart as best you can. You can use the information you collected on pages 18-19, the information I shared in the video today, and additionally, you are welcome to use a study Bible or a reliable online resource.

CLOSING PRAYER

DEAR GOD,

You are my God. I want to earnestly seek You. Thank You for being a God who fully forgives grievous sin and allows sinners to be in close relationship with You. I believe this in my head— help me believe this about You in my heart.

AMEN.

CLOSING RHYTHM

Read the entire passage aloud together. (I KNOW THIS IS WEIRD. Just be weird.)

DAY 1: CONTEXT OF THE CONTEXT

O God, you are my God; earnestly I seek you; my soul thirsts for you;
my flesh faints for you, as in a dry and weary land where there is no water.

Remember the info about David that I shared with you in the video? What part was the most shocking to you?

Keep in mind that these are real people. Sometimes we view Bible stories in a cartoonish way, and we forget that lots of the Bible is actually a historical account. (Side note: One of the reasons we can trust the Bible is the unbiased way it shares about its "heroes." Traditionally, David is one of the most loved and best known heroes in the Bible, and yet the text does not avoid talking about some of the horrific things he and his family did! Though God will generously forgive sin, He never overlooks it—and the Bible doesn't either.)

If you remember from the group session, Psalm 63 is a poem or song used for worship. However, the passages in 2 Samuel that likely give us context behind the psalm are a different genre: historical narrative. Historical narrative is written for the purpose of informing the audience of history through memorable storytelling.[2]

Today, I'm going to have you take a look at David's past and what happened before he was in the wilderness of Judah writing Psalm 63. We'll observe a few small pieces of text together because they create context for the context—the sin that prompted some of the drama that sent him into the wilderness.

READ 2 SAMUEL 11.

Take a look at verse 1. Where was David supposed to be? Where was he actually?

What is the first sin David commits? How does it escalate?

Take a look at verse 27. How does God feel about David's actions?

God hates sin not simply because it's bad but because it's bad for us. God knows the things David has done hurt and will hurt people. Who has been hurt so far?

Though there are always a lot of people who will tell a king or someone in power exactly what they desire to hear, Nathan was a prophet who had a history of speaking the difficult truth to

King David. Reread 2 Samuel 12:1-13 looking specifically at how Nathan spoke the truth to David on God's behalf.

How might you expect a person in power to respond when confronted in this way?

What is David's response to being confronted? What does this reveal about his character?

READ PSALM 51.

What does the superscription say?

Underline every reference to sin. Based on these observations, how does David view his sin?

Most of the time when David references his sin, he asks God to do something to that sin. Circle a few of these things. (For example, "Have mercy" and "blot out" in verse 1.)

Let's connect all of this back to Psalm 63. As you read, Psalm 51:11 says, "Cast me not away from your presence, and take not your Holy Spirit from me." Remember that David knows the same biblical principle we know: sin keeps us from God. David does not want to be separated from God, though he's sinned and has deeply offended God. But David knows another biblical principle as well: "A broken and a contrite heart, O God, you will not despise" (Ps. 51:17). In other words, God will not look down upon a person who truly desires to turn from his or her sinful ways. (Isn't that good news?) Through God's generous and undeserved forgiveness, David is able to be in right relationship with Him again.

For this reason, a very sinful man who has, frankly, messed up big time, is able to proclaim tenderly from a wilderness, "O God, _____ are _____ God" (Ps. 63:1).

How do these words impact you now that we better understand the cost of saying them?

What do these words teach us about God?

DEAR GOD,

Oh God, despite our sin, You allow us to say, "You are my God." Though You will never overlook our sin and pretend it doesn't happen, You are somehow willing to forgive what anyone else would call unforgivable. Thank You for the shocking togetherness of the gospel.

AMEN.

CLOSING RHYTHM

Read the entire passage aloud, or listen to one of the Psalm 63 songs. May it prompt you to worship God in a new way!

Take your time here and spread this out over two days.

DAYS 2-3: EAGERLY SEEKING

O God, you are my God; earnestly I seek you; my soul thirsts for you; my flesh faints for you, as in a dry and weary land where there is no water.

A few years ago, I was hosting a Mother's Day brunch. There were lots of details to manage, but despite the long list of to-dos, I found myself disproportionately honing in on one weird detail: a butter dish. The problem? I didn't have one. I'd need to serve butter with the waffles, and for whatever reason, I didn't want to put the butter on another kind of plate. So, my sister and I went to the store to purchase a butter dish. Unfortunately, the store didn't have a butter dish. Unfortunately, the next 700 stores did not have a butter dish. At some point in the search, I started to get a crazy look in my eye, and my sister said, "Wow. You are really fixating on this butter dish." I shook my fist at the sky and said, "I WILL HAVE A BUTTER DISH IF IT'S THE LAST THING I DO!" To this day, I have no idea why I cared so much.

I finally found a butter dish (it was ugly, but whatever), and we headed back to my house to accomplish the actual work of preparing for the brunch. Imagine my horror when I plopped the top of the dish onto the fresh stick of butter and realized the top was too shallow for a standard stick of butter. The lid just sat atop the butter, leaving half of the stick exposed to the elements, and I slowly grasped that this eagerly-sought-for-dish was completely unable to do its ONE JOB: cover a stick of butter. I can't remember if I flew into a fit of rage or into a fit of hysterical laughter, but I do remember that I spent the next two years shaving the top layer off every stick of butter I placed in the dish so it would fit before finally donating the cursed dish to a thrift store so it could ruin someone else's life.

side note: To this day, when I fixate on a detail and can't let go of it, my sister will say, "Are you butter-dishing?"

Here's the point: I eagerly sought that butter dish. I was desperate and determined to find that butter dish, and I lavishly spent my time and energy finding it.

> Do you have a story of eagerly seeking? Have you ever been so determined to have something that you abandoned all other concerns to get it?

Since we spent so much time in context (C) yesterday, today we're going to do the rest of the recipe (OIA) for the part of verse 1 that says, "earnestly I seek you."

OBSERVATION: WHAT DOES IT SAY?

One of the easiest ways to observe the text is to look up the definitions of the words. I especially love to look up the original language definition! (More on that later.) The original language word for "earnestly seek" is this:

| שָׁחַר **shâchar** *(shaw-khar′)* a primitive root; properly, to dawn, i.e. (figuratively) be (up) early at any task (with the implication of earnestness); by extension, to search for (with painstaking):—(do something) betimes, enquire early, rise (seek) betimes, seek diligently) early, in the morning).[3]

In the (slightly confusing) definition, we can see a few ideas repeated:

1. seeking/searching diligently (*diligent* means "characterized by steady, earnest, and energetic effort"[4])

2. the morning

> Take a moment to circle words in the definition that relate to either of those things.

Based on the definition, we better understand David's desire to find the Lord: It's something that gets him out of bed early in the morning! Have you seen the T-shirts that say, "Only a morning person on December 25"? The principle behind that shirt helps us understand verse 1 a bit better: Something has to be pretty awesome if we're willing to get up early for it. Can you think of something that would get you out of bed early? (I once got up at 4:30 a.m. in order to camp out at a new Chick-fil-A for the chance of winning a year's supply of chicken. It's a kind of lame story for another time.)

> Take some time to write a shortened version of the definition for "earnestly seek" on your copy of Psalm 63 just above the words. I wrote all of my definitions in light blue pen, but you can do whatever makes sense to you.

INTERPRETATION: WHAT DOES IT MEAN?

What does it mean that David is so excited in his search for the Lord? What is it about the Lord that makes David excitedly take on a "morning person" persona? I think the clue rests in the first part of the verse that we discussed earlier this week: "O God, you are my God." This part of the verse is all about relationship, and yesterday, when we dove deeper into David's context, we realized that this relationship is completely undeserved. By all accounts, David should be separate from God, but he isn't. God is able to see David's sin completely, yet forgive it fully and continue to be in relationship with him. David knows this is good news—not just in a responsible church way, but in a Christmas morning way.

> Let's interpret this verse with another verse. First John 4:19 says, "We love because he first loved us." Rewrite the verse below and then label one part of the verse "cause" and another part "effect." What causes what?

> Now, do the same for the first part of verse 1: "O God, you are my God; earnestly I seek you." Rewrite the verse below and then label one part of the verse "cause" and another part "effect." What causes what?

> David's relationship with God ("you are my God") provokes the seeking ("earnestly I seek you"). Label this cause and effect on your Psalm 63 text so we won't forget it.

APPLICATION: HOW SHOULD THIS CHANGE THE WAY I THINK AND LIVE?

In the past, I would have read this definition of "earnestly seeking," probably skipped the interpretation part, and thought, well, I guess I need to get up early in the morning to read my Bible. I don't think that's ever a bad idea, but I don't think the point here is to make a New Year's resolution. Based on what we uncovered in interpretation, what makes David earnestly seek the Lord? (Is it his own will, hustle, or goal? Or is it something else?)

> Think about the context stuff from Day 1. What was the true barrier to David's relationship with the Lord? ⬅

David understood two crucial things: (1) the depth of his sin and (2) the magnitude of God's forgiveness. This undeserved gift from God provoked David to seek God eagerly. Similarly, when we understand the depth of our sin and the magnitude of God's forgiveness, we

Was it David's failure to get up early to spend time with God? Or was it something else?

it's God's

KINDNESS

TO US THAT

provokes

the seeking

earnestly seek Him. It's God's kindness to us that provokes the seeking, not our own hustle to be a good church girl or to check a box.

Do you long to see the Lord earnestly, like David? Then do as he did: examine the depth of your sin, repent, and take a close look at the magnitude of God's forgiveness. A practical way to do this is to confess all the thoughts, actions, and words that you know are against God's will or that bring you shame. Share it all with Him honestly and repent, like David did in Psalm 51. Then, remember how God responded to David: with utter forgiveness. Perhaps this Psalm of David will help you better understand the magnitude of God's forgiveness:

The Lord is merciful and gracious,
slow to anger and abounding in steadfast love.
He will not always chide,
nor will he keep his anger forever.
He does not deal with us according to our sins,
nor repay us according to our iniquities.
For as high as the heavens are above the earth,
so great is his steadfast love toward those who fear him;
as far as the east is from the west,
so far does he remove our transgressions from us.
As a father shows compassion to his children,
so the Lord shows compassion to those who fear him.
PSALM 103:8-13

The better we can understand this miracle, the more we will desire to seek the One who loves us so well. His kindness leads us to repentance—and then to seeking.

CLOSING PRAYER

DEAR GOD,

You are my God. I want to earnestly seek You. Help me understand the depth of my sin and the magnitude of Your forgiveness. Help me to be in awe over the undeserved gifts You lavish on me.

AMEN.

CLOSING RHYTHM

Read the above selection from Psalm 103 out loud. (Sometimes saying true things out loud helps our hearts realize they're true.)

DAY 4: MAP

O God, you are my God; earnestly I seek you; my soul thirsts for you;
my flesh faints for you, as in a dry and weary land where there is no water.

When I was in high school, my family went on a trip to San Francisco. We had a great time hanging out together, seeing Alcatraz, and eating our way through a giant bag of freshly baked fortune cookies. I loved every bit of it—except our walk across the Golden Gate Bridge. Here's why: I'm afraid of heights to the point that the top bunk on a set of bunk beds makes my palms sweaty. Whenever my husband has playfully picked me up and swung me around, I've been so terrified to have my feet leave the ground that I've cried and yelled at him. (Cute, right?) So, obviously, what was a casual walk across a famous bridge for the other members of my family was a scene from a horror movie for me. I clung to the inner railing and inched my way forward at the speed of .0000001 miles per hour, while my younger siblings were chasing one another along the mile-long and mile-high pathway. My sweet mom gently championed me through it: "You've got this, honey! We're getting closer! When we get across the bridge, we'll get you a Coke and we can sit and relax for a while before getting a ride back." I put all my hope in that ice cold Coke that awaited on solid ground.

Finally, we got to the other side, but Caroline's Personal Nightmare was far from over. Not only were there approximately zero restaurants, vending machines, or even a water fountain, there was also no transportation back over the bridge. We had to walk the mile back across the mile-high bridge. I thought I was going to pass out. My family stared at me with wide eyes, probably thinking, "Oh no, we have to watch Caroline make her way across the bridge like a terrified slug again." Dramatic, right?

This scene was what popped in my head when I started analyzing the second half of verse 1: "… my soul thirsts for you; my flesh faints for you, as in a dry and weary land where there is not water." On the Golden Gate Bridge, I was thirsty for the Coke, but primarily I was thirsty for rescue. I was faint because I wasn't sure I could keep putting one foot in front of the other. The dry and weary land wasn't a literal wilderness like David's, but it was a setting of great fear and confusion, as I suspect David's setting was.

Have you ever been thirsty, faint, or in a setting of great fear and confusion? What was the situation?

Today, we're going to take a closer look at David's likely "dry and weary land." Before we examine David's external state, take a moment to remember David's internal state. Emotionally and spiritually, what was going on with him? (Think back to the teaching video earlier this week, or skim 2 Samuel 13–15.)

Now, let's consider his likely physical plight. Read 2 Samuel 16:5 through the end of 2 Samuel 17, and as you do:

- Put a box around any location you see (this can be a city, river, or a general location like "beyond the summit") and take note of what happened in that location.

- Double underline any name and try to understand what their location is and what their role is in regard to David.

- Place a star over anything you see that might make David weary.

There are two main groups of people moving about in 2 Samuel: David's people and Absalom's people. Map David's locations and movements in red and Absalom's locations and movements in green.

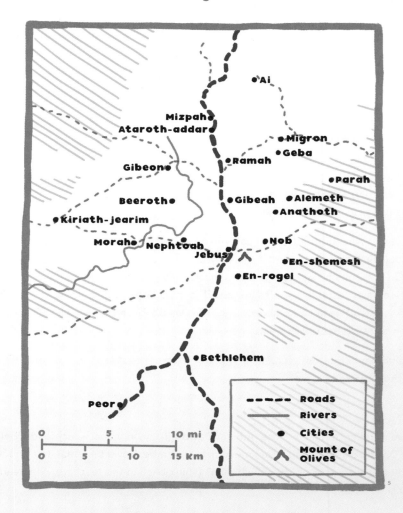

Here's a cool connection: Read 2 Samuel 16:14 and 2 Samuel 17:29 and underline any reference to weariness. Did you know the original language word for "weary" in these verses is the same word David uses in Psalm 63:1 for "thirst"?[6]

What kinds of things happened before and on this journey that might have made David weary?

Earlier this week, we paid attention to context to unpack David's reason behind the first part of verse 1, "O God, you are my God. Earnestly I seek you." Today, we've paid attention to context to unpack his reason behind the second part of verse 1, "My soul thirsts for you; my flesh faints for you, as in a dry and weary land where there is no water."

Based on all the context we've learned, do David's words seem more powerful to you? Why?

Why does context matter?

CLOSING PRAYER

DEAR GOD,

You are my God. I want to earnestly seek You. Thank You that I can do so by studying Your Word! When I am in a dry and weary land, help me thirst and faint for the proper thing: You. I know nothing else will satisfy.

AMEN.

CLOSING RHYTHM

Read Psalm 63 out loud.

THE ART OF PAYING ATTENTION

SESSION THREE

PSALM 63

1 *O God, you are my God; earnestly I seek you;*

my soul thirsts for you;

my flesh faints for you,

as in a dry and weary land where there is no water.

2 *So I have looked upon you in the sanctuary,*

beholding your power and glory.

3 *Because your steadfast love is better than life,*

my lips will praise you.

4 *So I will bless you as long as I live;*

in your name I will lift up my hands.

5 *My soul will be satisfied as with fat and rich food, and my mouth*

will praise you with joyful lips,

6 *when I remember you upon my bed,*

and meditate on you in the watches of the night;

7 *for you have been my help,*

and in the shadow of your wings I will sing for joy.

8 *My soul clings to you;*

your right hand upholds me.

9 *But those who seek to destroy my life*

shall go down into the depths of the earth;

10 *they shall be given over to the power of the sword;*

they shall be a portion for jackals.

11 *But the king shall rejoice in God;*

all who swear by him shall exult,

for the mouths of liars will be stopped.

WATCH

Watch the video and fill in the blanks before transitioning to the Discuss section.

Observation is the _____ of paying _____ .

DTR stands for _____ + _____ + _____ .

There are two places to look up definitions: ⟵ **Note-taking tip:** I like to write the
Original _____ dictionary and   definition really small over the
English _____ dictionary.   top of the word or in the margins,
depending on where there is space.

Note-taking tip: I like to
double underline themes and
A theme is an _____ that you see repeated.   write "Th" in the margins.

Note-taking tip: I like to highlight or
underline repeated words or phrases
Repetition is a _____   in the same color and number them.
or _____ that is repeated.

DTR is a good starting place to learn how to _____ _____ to the _____ .

DISCUSS

The second part of our COIA recipe is O, which stands for Observation. Observation means watching closely, paying attention, and asking, "What do I see here?" Observation is what we're doing when we notice our friends' mannerisms and favorite phrases. Observation is what we do when we realize the new cool thing is …. (Actually, I have no idea what the new cool thing is. Please tell me.) Observation is the art of paying attention.

But, then there's that sad human truth: our brains don't pay attention to boring things.[1] Sigh. Let's take a moment to consider what kinds of information your brain loves to gobble up like a plate of brownies—and what information feels more like an old, wilted salad. In short, let's take a moment to pay attention to how we pay attention. (Very meta.)

What fascinates you? What does "paying attention" look like for you in these situations?

What's the benefit to being an observant person in general?

What's the benefit to being an observant person specifically when it comes to the Bible?

To be good observers, we have to be invested in and fascinated by the information OR we have to be disciplined enough to invest our attention even when it makes our brain sleepy.

So I have looked upon you in the sanctuary,
beholding your power and glory.
PSALM 63:2

Before we observe the text with DTR, let's remember the first part of the recipe: Context.

Take a moment to discuss: What do you remember about David and this psalm?

Got the context wedged into your brain? Okay, let's DTR this thing.

Remember, when it comes to Bible reading, no one is grading you or judging whether or not you're a dummy, and you have total freedom to look up any word. I like to look up any word I'm only vaguely familiar with because it makes a HUGE difference in how well I'm able to pay attention to the text. I underline the words I want to look up as I'm reading, and when I'm done, I look them all up at once. I write the definition really small over the top of the word or in the margins, depending on where there is space.

There are two places I go when I'm looking up a word: an original language resource and then, if necessary, an English language resource. First, I use a tool like BlueLetterBible.org or StudyLight.org to get the original language definition. If it doesn't offer much help (sometimes, I'll look up a word, like "search," and Blue Letter Bible says, "It means 'to search,' and I'm like, 'You're not helping at all'"), I look up the word in an English dictionary.

D: DEFINITIONS

Use BlueLetterBible.org or StudyLight.org to look up Psalm 63:2. You'll need to use the "interlinear" tool. "Interlinear" sounds fancy, but it's simply a tool that allows you to examine the original words behind the English translation.[2] It's okay if this takes you a while. This is a new tool, and it will take some time to get used to it. This is a worthwhile investment of time! When you've figured it out, write a short version of the definition above each word.

To start you out on the right foot, I've placed the original language definition for "looked" below. Based on the context and tone of the text, I think it makes sense to write "contemplate (with pleasure)" above the word "looked." Go ahead and write that on your text.

חָזָה **châzâh** *(khaw-zaw')* a primitive root; to gaze at; mentally to perceive, contemplate (with pleasure); specifically, to have a vision of:—behold, look, prophesy, provide, see.[3]

With your group, track down the remaining definitions and write them down. You got this!

T: THEMES

A theme is an idea that comes up more than once. Keep the ideas of verse 2 in mind, and then read the rest of the text.

Do you notice any of the ideas from verse 2 repeated anywhere else in the text? If so, mark them.

I like to double underline themes and write "Th" in the margins. You might circle it, box it, put a squiggle under it—whatever makes sense to you! If you don't notice anything or find yourself overthinking it—that's okay! Just move on to the next thing.

Flip to page 141 to see a breakdown of the parts of a definition.

R: REPETITION

Repetition is a word or phrase that comes up a lot.

> **Do you notice any repetition within verse 2? Do you notice any of the words or phrases from verse 2 repeated anywhere else in the text? If so, mark them.**

I like to highlight or underline repeated words or phrases in the same color and number them. You might circle it, box it, put a squiggle under it—whatever makes sense to you!

Congratulations! You have officially DTR-ed verse 2 of Psalm 63! Don't panic if Scripture is not making you want to cartwheel at this exact moment. Structure isn't always glittery and loud and parade-like, but it's always necessary for the most delightful things. (I keep bringing that up because in this study, I not only want to equip you with how to study your Bible—I want to help you like it.) Even still, I hope you've found at least one thing that made you rub your chin like a genius professor on the verge of discovering a new element, or at least one thing that made you go, "Huh? Now what's that about?" Whatever that one bit of "sizzle" was, grab on to it! Share it with your group. Chew on it throughout your day like an Everlasting Gobstobber. (Willy Wonka? Anyone?)

Because here's the deal: We are playing a trick on your brain. MU-AH-HA-HA! (That's my evil laugh.) Our poor brains don't like to pay attention to boring things, but they're also really good at not realizing when something fascinating is before them. (Silly brains! We have to trick you, or you'll miss out on some really great stuff.) Structure—or knowing how to approach a boring thing—is a way to short-circuit the boringness. I hope DTR will help you pay attention, and I hope paying attention will help you become fascinated with the content. Good things are ahead, sister! Cue the confetti.

CLOSING PRAYER

DEAR GOD,

You are our God; we want to eagerly seek You. We want to thirst for You and Your Word. Make us hungry for You. Prompt our hunger for the right things—the God things.

AMEN.

CLOSING RHYTHM

Say verses 1 and 2 out loud five times. (I KNOW THIS IS WEIRD. Just be weird.)

DAY 1: "SO..."

So I have looked upon you in the sanctuary,
beholding your power and glory.

Sometimes tiny words can have a really big impact. In one of my favorite movies, *The Emperor's New Groove*, the villain Yzma threatens some children (as one does) and says, "Tell us where the talking llama is, and we'll burn your house to the ground!" Her lovable but oafish sidekick Kronk replies, "Er, don't you mean 'or'?" Yzma sighs in exasperation and corrects herself, "Tell us where the talking llama is, OR we'll burn your house to the ground!" The child she's threatening retorts, "Well, which is it? That seems like a pretty crucial conjunction."[4]

"A pretty crucial conjunction" is exactly what we have here in the word "so." It's a tiny word with a big impact. Here's the first part of the original language definition:

> כֵּן **kên** *(kane)* properly, set upright; hence (figuratively as adjective) just; but usually (as adverb or conjunction) rightly or so (in various applications to manner, time and relation; often with other particles)[5]

It's a bit difficult to sort through all the words in this definition, but according to smart Bible guy Eugene H. Merrill, this word "suggests in strong terms that the natural thing for David to do after recounting his complaint was to look to God."[6]

Do you see why "so" is a pretty crucial conjunction? Because it means something like, "Obviously!" or "Naturally!" Go ahead and write that above the word on your text. When you've done it, check this box: ☐

Remember that David says he is in a "dry and weary land," and we know from our context study that this is both a literal and a figurative reality for him. Take a moment to recap David's plight.

What kind of trouble is he carrying with him? Write a brief description below, remembering that this is the place where David "obviously" looks to the Lord.

We've observed this part of the text, but now let's dabble a bit with the next part of the COIA recipe: Interpretation. Interpretation means we come to the text, and we ask "What does it mean?" Let's consider what it means that David used this word "so." Re-read verses 1-2, but this time say, "So, obviously" instead of just "so," and then answer the following questions.

How does the original language meaning of the word "so" enhance my understanding of David's attitude toward God?

What does "so" reveal about David's faith?

Finally, let's dip a toe into the last part of the COIA recipe: Application. This is when we consider, "How does this impact the way I think and live?"

Is it a natural response for me to look to God when I'm in a dry and weary place?

What or who do I find myself naturally looking to when I'm in a desperate place?

Practically, what might it look like to "look to God" in my life? (Think of specific actions you might take or attitudes you might have.)

Are there any locations, relationships, or situations I'm currently enduring that feel like a "dry and weary land"?

How can David's response in a "dry and weary land" inform how I respond in my "dry and weary" place?

CLOSING PRAYER

DEAR GOD,

You are my God. I want to earnestly seek You. I want to thirst for You, to naturally look to You when I am in dry and weary places. Forgive me for the times I thirsted for lesser things, for the times when in my desperation I looked to others instead of You. Thank You for the truth of Your Word and for the challenge it is to my faith. Continue to help me understand it better and delight in it more.

AMEN.

CLOSING RHYTHM

Say verses 1 and 2 out loud five times. (YES, THIS IS WEIRD. Be weird.)

OBSERVATION is the art of paying ATTENTION

DAY 2: "i HAVE LOOKED UPON YOU iN THE SANCTUARY..."

So I have looked upon you in the sanctuary,
beholding your power and glory.

I want you to picture yourself as a die-hard groupie for some cool band. You're wearing one of their merch T-shirts, sitting in a room with walls covered by their posters. You're reading the lyrics to their newest song, and you are transfixed, curious, excited by the phrasings they chose, wondering almost obsessively, "WHAT DOES IT MEAN?" All your groupie friends come over, and you examine every syllable of every lyric and absolutely cannot settle down, even when your brother comes in and makes fun of you for being a nerd. "GET OUT OF HERE, HUNTER!" (Or whatever his name is. It's probably Hunter.)

Today, little groupies, I want to focus on the third part of the COIA recipe: Interpretation. This is when we come to the text and we ask, "What does it mean?" We'll talk more in-depth about interpretation in next week's group session, but for now, we're just die-hard groupies.

So, what in the world does David—who, might I remind you, is in the wilderness—mean by "sanctuary"? As a reminder, here's the definition:

> **Original Language Definition:**
> **שֹׁדֶק qôdesh** *(ko'-desh)* from H6942; a sacred place or thing; rarely abstract, sanctity:—consecrated (thing), dedicated (thing), hallowed (thing), holiness, (× most) holy (× day, portion, thing), saint, sanctuary.[7]

> **English Definition:**
> **sanctuary** a consecrated place[8]

We generally understand the word to be a specific, sacred (or "set apart"[9]) place. (Perhaps your church calls the place where everyone gathers for worship a "sanctuary.") But David isn't anywhere near any place that seems set apart for worship—or set apart for much of anything, for that matter! He's in a literal desert. (So much worse than a literal dessert.)

Write down some adjectives that describe a desert:

Now, for no good reason at all, think of your favorite dessert, and write down some adjectives that describe it:

Doesn't that sound delicious? We want God's word to be like a delicious feast to us—complete with dessert—especially when we feel as if we're in a spiritual desert.

Now that we're slightly hungry and have veered off course just a bit, it's a great time to remember we're reading a poem, not instructions or a letter or anything like that. In a poem, everything is not necessarily literal.

Keeping that in mind, what might David mean when talking about looking upon the Lord in a "sanctuary" when he's standing in a desert? WHAT DOES IT MEAN? Jot down some ideas below:

One of the best ways we can interpret a text and figure out what it means is to use Scripture. "Interpret Scripture using Scripture" is a super helpful framework, and there are two easy ways to do this:

1. Study Bibles list cross-references in the margins, which will show you other places in the Bible that communicate a similar idea.

2. A tool like BlueLetterBible.org will show you all the places where that same word is used.

By doing these two things, I was able to find another place in Scripture in which a person is in a wilderness and yet encountering a holy place.

Look up Exodus 3:5 and write it below. Which part of the Exodus 3:5 do you think is the word *qôdesh*? Circle or underline it.

Are you familiar with this story Read all of Exodus 3 so you'll have a feel for the context.

Perhaps Exodus 3:5 can help us understand Psalm 63:2 a bit better. See what connections you can make between the two verses and write them out below.

And just for fun, let's consider a bit of application. Today, in your life, what might be considered a "sanctuary" based on the way the idea is presented in these verses?

CLOSING PRAYER

DEAR GOD,

You are my God. I want to earnestly seek You. Help me develop a taste for the deliciousness of your Word, even when I feel as if I'm standing in a spiritual desert. Thank You for making the Bible intriguing and full of mystery! Will You help me better understand this idea of "sanctuary"? Will You bring the idea to my mind throughout the day so that I can meditate on and wonder about Your Word?

AMEN.

Whisper verses 1 and 2 creepily five times. (Just kidding, you can just say it regularly. Either way, I know it's weird. Embrace the weird.)

DAY 3: "...BEHOLDING YOUR POWER AND GLORY."

So I have looked upon you in the sanctuary,
beholding your power and glory.

Did you think any more about the idea of "sanctuary"? Does it have to be a specific place? What makes a place holy and set apart? Are there any other parts of Scripture or ideas that come into your head when you're thinking about this stuff?

Today we get to take it a step further and investigate what David does in this figurative "sanctuary": He beholds God's power and glory.

> **During this week's group session, you worked together to track down definitions of the words in this verse. Take a look at the definitions for "behold," "power," and "glory." You can rewrite them below if it helps."**

Here's one fun nuance I noticed. The original language definition for "looked up" implies joy (it means "to contemplate with pleasure"), and the original language definitions listed for "beholding" includes some references to joy, as well.

> **So, how is this joy a shift in tone from verse 1?**

You know what? I like that David didn't just "look" at God. That can feel pretty vague and unhelpful for us. Has anyone ever encouraged you to "look to God"? It sounds nice, but my internal response is always, "What does that even mean?" I don't like foggy, spiritual advice. But David isn't being vague here.

> **He's looking at God in specific ways, by beholding two of His characteristics: His _____ and _____.**

Something about "beholding [God's] power and glory" is a significant encouragement for David because it seems to lift his spirits and lift his language when he's in a very difficult place. Strangely, David is in a posture of joyful worship while being hated and hunted by his own son. Why? Because worship made him joyful. While he was in a dry and weary land, David looked to the Lord and considered God's power and God's glory, and this made all the difference.

> Why might these two God characteristics (power and glory) be especially helpful to a king who is (1) at risk of losing his throne to his son, (2) at risk of losing his life, and (3) far away from every comfort and sense of safety?

Let's focus in on the last part of the COIA recipe today: Application. This is when we consider how the text should change the way we think and live.

When we are in dry and weary places, we can also look to God. But this isn't a foggy, spiritual, ooey gooey thing with no foundation. This "looking" gets to be specific. We can zero in on specific characteristics of God. This is important because knowing what God is like is a game changer for life—it's the thing that offers us joy in weary places.

Here's an example: My family was in the adoption process for three years. It was really stressful financially, emotionally, and even logistically as we struggled to know how to make future plans when everything was so unknown. But in this dry and weary place, it always gave me great comfort and joy to remember God's provision (His ability to provide everything we need for a godly life; 2 Pet. 1:3) and omniscience (His ability to know everything even when I don't; Ps. 139:16). Over and over again through the weariness, I could say, "I have joyfully looked upon you in the empty nursery, beholding your provision and omniscience." Though that empty nursery was often an upsetting place, a place of spiritual dryness and weariness, looking to the Lord in a specific way produced genuine worship in my heart—and even joy— because it was so good to remember what He's really like based on what I read in the Bible, instead of what I often think He's like.

> What are some God characteristics that mean a lot to you? (Be sure these are characteristics that can be found in the Bible!) What are some specific "deserts" where those characteristics might be helpful and even produce joy?

CLOSING PRAYER

DEAR GOD,

You are my God; earnestly I seek You. My soul thirsts for You; my flesh faints for You, as in a dry and weary land where there is no water. So I have looked upon You in the _____, beholding Your _____ and _____. Because Your steadfast love is better than life, my lips will praise You.

AMEN.

CLOSING RHYTHM

Operatically sing verses 1 and 2 five times. (Or say it regularly. Whatever.)

DAY 4: CATCH UP + PLAY

Catch up on any parts of Days 1-3 that you missed, skimmed, or skipped.

Then, rewrite verses 1-2 however you'd like (make it pretty, make it ugly, make it whatever—no one is judging or grading you), and try to mentally "take a picture" of each word as you write so that you can commit it to memory. When you're done, say the two verses out loud ten times. (Yeah, it's kinda weird, but it helps.) Then give yourself a high-five—you have done great work this week!

WHAT DID HE MEAN BY THAT?

PSALM 63

1 *O God, you are my God; earnestly I seek you;*

my soul thirsts for you;

my flesh faints for you,

as in a dry and weary land where there is no water.

2 *So I have looked upon you in the sanctuary,*

beholding your power and glory.

3 *Because your steadfast love is better than life,*

my lips will praise you.

4 *So I will bless you as long as I live;*

in your name I will lift up my hands.

5 *My soul will be satisfied as with fat and rich food, and my mouth*

will praise you with joyful lips,

6 *when I remember you upon my bed,*

and meditate on you in the watches of the night;

7 *for you have been my help,*

and in the shadow of your wings I will sing for joy.

8 *My soul clings to you;*

your right hand upholds me.

9 *But those who seek to destroy my life*

shall go down into the depths of the earth;

10 *they shall be given over to the power of the sword;*

they shall be a portion for jackals.

11 *But the king shall rejoice in God;*

all who swear by him shall exult,

for the mouths of liars will be stopped.

WATCH

Watch the video and fill in the blanks before transitioning to the Discuss section.

It's _____ that really help us know God better.

God is honored when we genuinely desire to _____ Him.

What is the magic question for interpretation?

There are three tools for interpreting the text:

    1. S is for_____ .

    2. G is for_____ .

    3. C is for_____ .

It is so smart to interpret the Bible alongside other _____ .

DISCUSS

Before we get into the really good stuff, let's review the recipe. Together with your group, fill out the blanks, or, race to see who can fill them out first:

C is for _____

O is for _____   **Hint: DTR**

    In observation, we can _____ _____ _____ the text.

I is for _____   **Hint: SGC**

    In interpretation, we can _____ _____ _____ the text.

A is for _____

Chat with your group: Is the recipe starting to make sense to you? If you accidentally lost this book, would you be able to remember the recipe with only the power of your brain? (Any answer is totally fine, and I'm not awarding any trophies or anything to people who've already nailed it. The only point for this is to check in with one another and to be forced to process how much is stuck in your brain.)

The value of a recipe is less about making sure a cook makes a dish the "right" way and more about equipping him or her to be successful in making a dish. Our Bible reading recipe is the same way! Is this always and forever the "right" way to read? Not necessarily. But is this recipe able to equip you to be successful in your reading? Totally!

The truth is that Bible reading can be a very overwhelming thing.

Do you ever feel dumb when you read the Bible? How can we combat these feelings?

Let's chat about interpretation for a bit:

What does it mean to interpret Scripture with "my-crush-wrote-me-a-note" delight?

Why should we seek to do interpretation in community when we can?

What does SGC stand for?

Do you have access to a study Bible? (A study Bible is a Bible that has cross-references, which are the tiny references in the margin, and other helpful study tools, like context information at the beginning of each book.) If not, spend some time today figuring out how to access one online or make plans to purchase one.

Now, let's jump into some study:

OBSERVATION

David says, "Your steadfast love is better than life." This Hebrew term "steadfast love" is jam-packed with meaning. We'll get into it more this week, but for now, look up the original language definition together and discuss.

How is this term more substantial than the way we use the word "love"?

YOUR **stead-fast love** IS BETTER THAN LIFE

INTERPRETATION (SGC)

In my study Bible, this cross-reference is listed next to "steadfast love"[1]:
Psalm 69:16. Look up the verse and write it below.

How does this cross-reference help you understand the original verse?

Is there anything you're curious about in this verse and in the original verse?

Look up the following cross-references and write them in the space provided. How do
these cross-referenced verses help you understand the original verse? Where do you
see the gospel? What are you curious about in these verses and in the original verse?

- "as long as I live": Psalm 104:33; 146:2

- "name": Psalm 20:1,5

- "lift up my hands": Psalm 28:2

CLOSING PRAYER

DEAR GOD,

*You are our God. Help us understand more about Your steadfast love. Is it really better than
life? Help us grasp this, so that we can bless You as long as we live.*

AMEN.

CLOSING RHYTHM

Read the entire passage aloud together. (Again, I KNOW THIS IS WEIRD. Just be weird.)

DAY 1: COi

Because your steadfast love is better than life, my lips will praise you.
So I will bless you as long as I live; in your name I will lift up my hands.

Today we'll be dabbling a bit in context, observation, and interpretation. I've noticed that sometimes, once I've started really immersing myself in the text, the different parts of the recipe will ebb and flow rather than be totally regimented. That's fine! The point is to know and love God and His Word more—not perfectly execute a recipe. (But you may want to see if you can tell what we're doing when!)

Okay, let's dive in and take a closer look at the phrase that inspired the name of this study. Fill in the blank:

Your steadfast love is _____ _____ _____

I mean, whoa. Just so we're clear, here's the original language definition for "life":

חַי chay *(khah'-ee)* from H2421; alive; hence, raw (flesh); fresh (plant, water, year), strong; also (as noun, especially in the feminine singular and masculine plural) life (or living thing), whether literally or figuratively:— age, alive, appetite, (wild) beast, company, congregation, life(-time), live(-ly), living (creature, thing), maintenance, merry, multitude, (be) old, quick, raw, running, springing, troop.[2]

Circle the parts of the definition that best fit in the context of "life" in this verse. Write a small definition on your text. When you've done it, check this box: ☐

Then, write those words on the right side of the line under "life."

God's Love	Life

Remember the original language definition for "steadfast love" that you looked up in the group discussion? Flip back to it, and write the definition on the left side of the chart above.

David has created a memorable comparison, and I'm hoping the chart above will help us better grasp the comparison. He genuinely believes that God's love is better than being alive. It seems to me that this is an unusual thing for a person in David's position to say. Let's take a minute to refresh ourselves on David's likely situation (context):

What is David's position in the culture?

What do you think his lifestyle is like?

Despite all of that, where is David? Why is he there?

How is this environment different from his home?

If he's found, what will likely happen?

Now, David is no stranger to near-death experiences. In fact, the previous king, Saul, tried to kill David several times. Even before that, when David was a young shepherd, he had to ward off lions and bears from his sheep, and he volunteered to stand against the fearsome Goliath. (Remember that story? This is a brave dude!) Even still, this particular plight is different because of who is trying to kill him. It's not some enemy or rival—it's his own son.

> **Read 2 Samuel 13:37-39. Absalom has just killed his half-brother Amnon, and while David is mourning Amnon, Absalom flees. Despite what Absalom has done, how does David feel about Absalom?**

Of course, we've already learned a bit about how layered this conflict is, but it's safe to say that emotionally, this must be a very painful situation for David.

> **Read 2 Samuel 16:5-14. What stands out to you in these verses?**

Isn't it strange for a king (or anyone) to allow someone to yell curses, throw stones, and fling dust at him?

> **Why does he allow this? What does this tell us about David's emotional state?**

> **Consider everything you know about David's physical and emotional context. What are some things a person would understandably desire in that situation and might ask the Lord for? Write that list to the right of the line under "wilderness desires."**

David's Desires	Wilderness Desires

Interestingly, we don't see David asking for things, and we only see him wanting one thing: "earnestly I seek you; my soul thirsts for you; my flesh faints for you" (v. 1).

Look at the text, and circle "you" and "your" every time you see it in verses 1-3. Then, write "YOU" to the left of the line under "David's desires."

In this emotionally and literally dry and weary land, David looks to the Lord, considers His power and glory (v. 2), and declares, "Your steadfast love is better than life" (v. 3). Glance back over the two charts from today's study and spend some time wrestling with this:

Why does David believe God's love is so much better than everything else—not just in a spiritual, churchy way, but in a gritty, real-life, wilderness way? Is this perspective something you've genuinely encountered in someone else or in yourself before? If you like, take some time to journal your response.

Finally, take a closer look at verse 3. The belief that God's love is better than life requires a response.

What is the response?

CLOSING PRAYER

DEAR GOD,

You are my God. I want to earnestly seek You, I want to thirst for You, I want to faint for You. Is Your love really better than life? Help me know You better so that I can be convinced of this, too.

AMEN.

CLOSING RHYTHM

Read Psalm 63 or listen to it on an audio Bible or through one of the Psalm 63 songs we've discovered. And yeah—I know I keep saying this,

DAY 2: WORD STUDY: STEADFAST LOVE

Because your steadfast love is better than life, my lips will praise you.
So I will bless you as long as I live; in your name I will lift up my hands.

When my youngest son joined our family, it took about two seconds for my daughter to become completely smitten with him. She hovered over him constantly and perpetually gritted her teeth saying things like, "I want to squeeze him!" and "I just want to eat him up!" She's heard me say this kind of thing, because I've been known to say my children are delicious and yummy and I want to eat them for breakfast. Even still, Adelaide said it so often and with such passion that I said to my husband, "Do you think she really wants to eat him?"

Don't worry, I'm not raising a cannibal. The truth is that this phenomenon Adelaide and I both experience in response to cute babies is a normal thing—but our language doesn't have a word for it. But in Tagalog, a language spoken by some Filipinos (people from the Philippines), they call it *gigil*. "*Gigil* refers to the trembling or gritting of the teeth in response to a situation that overwhelms your self-control. It's been commonly described as an irresistible urge to squeeze something cute."[5]

Have you ever experienced an overwhelming urge to squeeze something cute? Maybe puppies? Or baby pandas?

Gigil is one of many examples of language falling short. English simply doesn't offer all the words we need to fully describe our experiences. In fact, English doesn't offer all the words the original writers of the Bible used. Did you know that when the Bible was first translated into English, the original manuscripts (Hebrew, Aramaic, and Greek) used about 11,280 words, but the English translation only used about 6,000 different words?[6] Simply put, our language has limits. This is another reason why careful study is so important. We don't want to miss the good stuff just because we don't have the perfect English word for it!

Real talk: We don't have the perfect English word for a very important part of Psalm 63— "steadfast love."

Yesterday, we wrestled with why God's steadfast love is better than life. (And it's okay to still be wrestling with that!) Today, let's put God's steadfast love under a microscope. What is it shaped like? What is it made out of? To do this, we're going to do a word study of the original language word, חֶסֶד. A transliteration of the word (meaning, a word from a different language written in letters the reader can understand and pronounce) is checed or hesed.

We've dabbled a bit into this word already, so flip back to the group session from this week, and write below everything you know about hesed:

Use a concordance like BlueLetterBible.org to look up other times when this word is used in the Old Testament. (Why the Old Testament? Because the New Testament was written in Greek, not Hebrew! Hesed is a Hebrew word.) Here's a trick for word studies like this: Strong's Concordance, which is what most online resources use, gives every original language word a unique code. (You may have noticed this when you've looked up original language words with your group.) You can simply enter the code into the search box to see all the times when that precise word was used. (This is more effective than searching for the English words "steadfast love" since it may not have been translated the same way each time.) The code for hesed is H2617.

Once you've found a few options that seem to use hesed the same way it's used in Psalm 63:3, write them below:

Now, let's look up Psalm 63:3 in other translations. (A website like BibleHub.com will allow you to glance over a bunch of translations at one time.)

In the space below, write down as many translations of "steadfast love" as you can.

This will help us grasp how many English words have been attempted to properly communicate the idea of hesed as it's used in this verse.

Finally, since the translation we've been using in this study translates hesed "steadfast love," let's look up "steadfast" to ensure we fully understand what the translators were trying to communicate.

Write the definition below:

Now, in your own words, use the information you collected to write a brief description of your understanding of this word: steadfast.

How does what you've learned about this word help you understand its meaning in Psalm 63?

Now that you have a better grasp of *hesed* or "steadfast love," write a summary of the definition above the word on your text. Check this box when you've done it: ☐. Great work today!

HOW TO DO A WORD STUDY

1. Dictionary: Look up the original language definition of the word. If there are several definitions, try to discern which definition best fits based on the context. If there are words in the definition that confuse you, look them up in an English dictionary.

2. Concordance: Use a concordance to find places in the Bible where this word is used in the same way.

3. Other translations: Take the original verse and read it in other translations. How do other translations translate the word?

4. Summarize: Based on the information you've taken in, summarize the meaning of the word.

5. Reflect: How does what you've learned about the word help you to understand its meaning in the passage?

CLOSING PRAYER

DEAR GOD,

You are my God. I want to earnestly seek You, and I want to better understand Your steadfast love. My head understands that it is better than life, but I want my heart to understand it, too.

AMEN.

CLOSING RHYTHM

Read Psalm 63 or listen to it via an audio Bible or through one of the Psalm 63 songs we've discovered. You won't regret pressing on in this habit!

DAY 3: APPLICATION

Because your steadfast love is better than life, my lips will praise you.
So I will bless you as long as I live; in your name I will lift up my hands.

Since we've dabbled a bit in COI, let's spend today on A, application. Application is the final part of the recipe, in which we consider a text and ask, "How should this change the way I think or live?" Grab a piece of paper and cover up the page below this next question so you can attempt to think through application without outside influence. Then, read verses 3 and 4 out loud.

Do you have any ideas about how we might apply these verses to our lives? Jot your ideas down below.

I suspect the most obvious application is to take David's actions and make them our actions: "My lips should praise God. I should bless him as long as I live. In his name, I should lift up my hands." This is, of course, not a bad idea by any stretch of the imagination. But too hastily applying it this way misses a crucial aspect of the verse.

Can you figure out what that is?

Circle the word "because." What role does this word play in this verse?

What motivates David's worship?

Knowing this, what should motivate our worship?

Earlier this week, we more fully unpacked "steadfast love" or *hesed*.

Knowing what you know about *hesed*, do David's beliefs and worshipful response make more sense to you? Explain.

After all, a grasp of hesed comes before the worship. If we want to worship like David, we need to look at God like David looks at God.

Here's a great application question for you: How can you get a David-level grasp of God's *hesed*?

For some biblical ideas about this, read 1 John 5:14; Colossians 1:9; Ephesians 3:17-19; and 2 Peter 1:3. Feel free to jot them down below. Then, using the "Closing Prayer" space, craft a prayer to the Lord based on what you've learned from those verses.

CLOSING PRAYER

DEAR GOD,

_____

_____

_____

_____

_____

_____

_____

_____

_____

_____

_____

AMEN.

CLOSING RHYTHM

Read Psalm 63, listen to it on an audio Bible or through one of the Psalm 63 songs we've discovered, or speak it to God as a prayer. Whenever we don't know what to pray, we are free to borrow God's words and pray them back to Him!

DAY 4: iNTERPRETATiON—WORSHiP

Because your steadfast love is better than life, my lips will praise you.
So I will bless you as long as I live; in your name I will lift up my hands.

A large percentage of text this week involves worship. David believes that God's steadfast love is better than life, and this belief leads him to worship by praising God with his lips, blessing God as long as he lives, and lifting up his hands in the Lord's name.

So, what is worship? As we close out the week, we are going to spend our time interpreting this concept, asking "What does it mean?"

To start, write down everything you associate with "worship."

"Worship" is a churchy word for sure, and if we're not careful, we can think "worship" means singing in a church service. This, of course, is a part of worship, but there's much more. Worship can take place at any time or place (remember, David is in the wilderness!), and worship involves the whole self.

Skim Psalm 63 and write down every phrase that hints at David's worship of God:

Remember, interpretation involves SGC—Scripture, Gospel, and Curiosity. Let's use a combination of all three of these things to take a closer look at what some other parts of the Bible reveal about worship.

Look up each verse and write it below. Then, answer the questions. As you interact with the verses, feel free to write anything helpful in the margins of your Psalm 63 text.

Matthew 15:8-9

- **According to this verse, what makes worship worthless?**

- **What part of the "whole self" is revealed as a part of worship in this passage?**

- **How does this reveal the gospel?**

Romans 12:1

- What part of the "whole self" is revealed as a part of worship in this passage?

- What do you think it means to be a "living sacrifice"?

- How does this concept reflect the gospel?

Romans 12:2

- What part of the "whole self" is revealed as a part of worship in this passage?

- John Piper says, "When we worship—right worship, good worship, pleasing worship—depends on a right mental grasp of the way God really is."[7] (Read John 2:23-24 if you want to see the passage he's referencing.) How is that concept also present in Romans 12:2?

- How can Bible study be an act of worship that involves your whole self?

CLOSING PRAYER

DEAR GOD,

You are my God. Earnestly I seek You! I desire to look upon You, to behold Your power and glory. I desire to know deep in my bones that Your steadfast love is better than life, so that my lips will praise You and my whole self will match its praise. I want to bless You as long as I live; in your name I will lift up my hands.

AMEN.

CLOSING RHYTHM

Read Psalm 63, listen to it on an audio Bible or through one of the Psalm 63 songs we've discovered. May it stir up worship in your heart!

THE STORY OF HUNGER

PSALM 63

1 *O God, you are my God; earnestly I seek you;*

my soul thirsts for you;

my flesh faints for you,

as in a dry and weary land where there is no water.

2 *So I have looked upon you in the sanctuary,*

beholding your power and glory.

3 *Because your steadfast love is better than life,*

my lips will praise you.

4 *So I will bless you as long as I live;*

in your name I will lift up my hands.

5 *My soul will be satisfied as with fat and rich food, and my mouth*

will praise you with joyful lips,

6 *when I remember you upon my bed,*

and meditate on you in the watches of the night;

7 *for you have been my help,*

and in the shadow of your wings I will sing for joy.

8 *My soul clings to you;*

your right hand upholds me.

9 *But those who seek to destroy my life*

shall go down into the depths of the earth;

10 *they shall be given over to the power of the sword;*

they shall be a portion for jackals.

11 *But the king shall rejoice in God;*

all who swear by him shall exult,

for the mouths of liars will be stopped.

WATCH

Watch the video and fill in the blanks before transitioning to the Discuss section.

The Bible contains 66 books, but it's also important to know that it's _____
_____ _____.

THE STORY OF HUNGER

Mark the various events and Scripture passages on the timeline as you watch the video.[1]

Movement 1: Creation

Movement 2: Fall

Movement 3: Pursuit

Movement 4: Jesus

Movement 5: Church

Movement 6: The Return of the King + New Creation

DISCUSS

How would you define hunger? After you decide on your own definition, look it up in a dictionary.

How do you act when you're hungry? What does hunger cause you to do or say?

What kinds of cravings do you experience? First discuss food cravings, and then discuss other cravings (i.e., craving approval, friendship, success, etc.).

Have you ever heard the Bible referred to as one story?

What part of the story most stands out to you?

Humans have always been looking for things to satisfy their cravings. Based on what you heard in the story, what has God always been doing?

APPLICATION

We've already discussed cravings we personally experience. Based on The Story of Hunger, what is the lesson for that craving? What is the good news for your hungry soul?

Challenge for the week: Pay attention to the cravings in your life.

CLOSING PRAYER

DEAR GOD,

You are our God. Earnestly we seek You! Our souls thirst—and we now know they thirst for You. Even as we crave lesser things, we know You are the One who can satisfy our souls as with fat and rich food. Help us remember that truth!

AMEN.

CLOSING RHYTHM

Read verse 5 aloud together.

DAY 1: OBSERVATION

My soul will be satisfied as with fat and rich food,
and my mouth will praise you with joyful lips.

Today, we're going to observe the text, which means we will pay close attention to it and ask "What does it say?" As I challenged you in the group session, I want you to continue to observe your life in the same way—pay attention to it and ask "What does it say?" or more specifically for our purposes, "What cravings do I observe in my life?" You'll want to make sure you have some colorful pens and/or highlighters nearby, and that you have access to an original language dictionary, like BlueLetterBible.org. Let's do this!

PAY ATTENTION

One great way to pay attention to the text is to attempt to write it in your own words. Paraphrase verse 5 in the space below.

David mentions two things in this verse: satisfaction and praise. Take a look at the verses that come before verse 5. What prompts David's satisfaction and praise?

Now, let's DTR the text:

DEFINITIONS

Look up the original language definition for "satisfied," and write it below:

Are there any other words you'd like to look up? Do that now. Remember, you are welcome to use a regular dictionary if the original language dictionary doesn't offer any new information. Write the definitions on your text, and when you've done that, check this box: ☐. Yay!

THEMES AND REPETITION

If you'll think back to when we first chatted about observation, we said a theme is an idea that comes up more than once, and repetition is a word or phrase that comes up more than once. I'm going to get wild and crazy and take some liberty with this part of the recipe. Instead of our traditional theme/repetition observation, let's observe a technique that comes up more than once: sensory language.

Throughout the Psalms, we see lots of sensory language—that is, language about the five senses: sight, smell, hearing, taste, and touch.

Read all of Psalm 63 and mark two things:

1. Any sensory language you see

I highlighted this in orange, but do what makes sense to you! Be sure to add it to your "key" so you know what the markings mean later.

2. Any part of self (i.e., "mouth" or "soul")

I boxed these in orange highlighter, but do what makes sense to you.

Sensory language is helpful when we want someone who wasn't there to understand how we felt. This is a great time to remember the context: David is in the wilderness. But he's not trying to explain his body's experience in the wilderness—he's trying to explain his soul's experience in the wilderness. This makes the language especially interesting because we don't have words to explain how our souls feel—we have to borrow words from other senses.

The sensory language in Psalm 63 tends to fall into two categories: the desert experience and the satisfaction experience. Try to categorize the words you've marked in this way.

Desert Experience	Satisfaction Experience

Now that we've observed this verse, take some time to observe your life, or more specifically, your soul. What is it experiencing? Record your observations, and feel free to use sensory language like David to put words to what is probably a wordless experience!

CLOSING PRAYER

Follow David's lead and write a prayer to God about the state of your soul. You are always welcome to borrow words from Psalm 63 if you can't find the words on your own.

DEAR GOD,

_____

_____

AMEN.

CLOSING RHYTHM

Read Psalm 63 or listen to it via an audio Bible or through one of the Psalm 63 songs we've discovered. Maybe it will sound fresh and new as you listen today!

DAY 2: INTERPRETATION (SGC)

My soul will be satisfied as with fat and rich food,
and my mouth will praise you with joyful lips.

Last week, we talked about how God's steadfast love (*hesed*) prompts David to worship. Yesterday we observed that this week's verse reveals another prompting for worship: satisfaction. Today we are going to dip our toe into interpretation, which is when we come to the text and we ask, "What does it mean?" What does it really mean for David's soul to be satisfied and prompted to worship, even in a desert?

To do this, we'll follow the recipe for interpretation, and use SGC (Scripture, Gospel, Curiosity) to help us get a better grasp on this curious verse. You'll be flipping around in your Bible a bit, so take a minute to stretch your page-flipping muscles, and then let's get at it.

SCRIPTURE

Let's take a look at the cross-reference[2] for this verse: Psalm 36:8. Write this verse below.

This verse is all about feasting on the Lord's abundance. I especially love the phrase "river of your delights." It's such good news that God offers delight! Is that difficult for you to remember?

Playback the tape a bit and read Psalm 36:7. Write it below.

Do you see any familiar words or phrases?

Now read Psalm 36:5,10. What word(s) is repeated?

Based on these verses, what connections can you make between *hesed* and satisfaction?

Let's look a little bit closer at this connection. Psalm 107:9 says, "For he satisfies the longing soul, and the hungry soul he fills with good things."

This isn't a cross-reference, just an awesome verse
I accidentally came across! Isn't it powerful?

In this verse, the word "for" functions kind of like the word "because." In other words, verse 9 is saying "Because of _____, he satisfies the longing soul …"

Play back the tape a bit to Psalm 107:8. What is it that prompts this satisfaction?

Now read Psalm 107:15,21,31. What do they all say?

According to David, who wrote Psalm 63, and the psalmist who wrote Psalm 107, who is the source of satisfaction? Specifically, how are we satisfied?

GOSPEL

Did you know that Jesus also talked about spiritual hunger and satisfaction? Look up Matthew 5:6 and write it below.

This is from the famous Sermon on the Mount. According to Jesus, is it good to hunger and thirst for righteousness (which means to be free from sin)? Why?

Do you ever hunger to be free from sin?

If you remember from The Story of Hunger in the group session, Jesus is the Bread of life. The part of the text when He says this, John 6, is a really curious passage, and it's helpful to know that all this teaching on bread comes on the heels (bread pun) of feeding the 5,000. Do you remember that Bible story? Jesus had miraculously filled the bellies of a huge crowd with a little boy's lunch, and the crowd came after Him the next day, looking for something more. Take a look at the good but strange news Jesus had for them in John 6:48-51:

> *I am the bread of life. Your fathers ate the manna in the wilderness, and they died. This is the bread that comes down from heaven, so that one may eat of it and not die. I am the living bread that came down from heaven. If anyone eats of this bread, he will live forever. And the bread that I will give for the life of the world is my flesh.*
> **JOHN 6:48-51**

According to Jesus, who is the source of satisfaction? How does He satisfy?

Let me spell it out a bit since this is such a weird idea: Jesus' flesh, given for the life of the world, offers life forever. True satisfaction. Why would Jesus' flesh offer satisfaction?

How does Jesus' flesh equip a believer to say, "My soul will be satisfied as with fat and rich food, and my mouth will praise you with joyful lips"?

What connections can you make between *hesed* and Jesus' flesh?

CURIOSITY

In this searching today, did anything pique your curiosity? Maybe you wanted to look a bit more at Psalm 36, Psalm 107, or John 6. (There's a LOT of cool and crazy stuff in John 6!) Maybe there was a word you wanted to look up and dig into. Take the time to chase your curiosity and wrestle through the confusing places.

CLOSING PRAYER

DEAR GOD,

You are my God; earnestly I seek You. Thank You that through Jesus' work on the cross, believers can have satisfied souls. My mouth will praise You will joyful lips!

AMEN.

CLOSING RHYTHM

Read Psalm 63 or listen to it via an audio Bible or through one of the Psalm 63 songs we've discovered. May it lead you to worship!

DAYS 3-4: APPLICATION

*My soul will be satisfied as with fat and rich food,
and my mouth will praise you with joyful lips*

Pretend you're a parent, and fill in the blank: "Don't eat that. You'll ruin your _____." We've probably all heard it: "No brownies before dinner—that'll ruin your appetite." "No candy before dinner—that'll ruin your appetite." Why are parents so concerned about our appetites? Is it really that big of a deal for a kid to fill up on brownies and not be hungry for dinner?

Listen, I really thought I'd be a cool parent who let my kids eat cookies for dinner. (Mainly because I want cookies for dinner.) But let me tell you how that goes:

Cookie Kid eats cookies. Cookie Kid's body won't get the nutrients he needs to sustain him and to help his body function in his best interest. Instead of the needed nutrients, he'll get lots of sugar, which will likely cause him to misbehave. (It's difficult to control a sudden influx of unexpected energy!) He'll morph into a hyper human tornado until he dramatically crashes. But don't think the crash indicates he's in for a good night's sleep—no way. He'll sleep fitfully because his body simply doesn't have what it needs to offer good rest. Yikes.

Parents aren't being kill-joys when they caution kids against ruining their appetites. They just know how this plays out, and they want to protect the kids (okay, and themselves) from a roller coaster ride that starts out fun and ends up with crying, time-outs, and nightmares.

Spiritual cravings can have the same impact as physical cravings. Sometimes we'll reach for something that ruins our appetite for God.[3]

> Can you think of anything that might ruin your spiritual appetite?

> Read Psalm 78. It's a little long and there are some really confusing parts, but I think it will help us as we apply Psalm 63:5 to our lives. When you're done reading it, write "I did it!" below:

> Way to go! Thanks for doing that. I know it may have felt like running a few laps at the gym. Are there any specific parts of Psalm 78 that got your heart rate up and grabbed your attention? Write them below.

Remember The Story of Hunger from this week's group session? Psalm 78 is like a miniature Story of Hunger—people craving what will not satisfy while the God of satisfaction continues to display His wonders, His holiness, and His mercy. This Psalm is a historical psalm, which means it was written so that generations of Israelites would remember not just God's faithfulness, but their faithlessness. (I love that these generations were taught to be so honest in their reflection of themselves!) One verse in particular that chilled me was verse 19: "They spoke against God, saying, 'Can God spread a table in the wilderness?'" You can tell they are asking this question in a sneering, sarcastic way.

How do you think David would have responded to that question based on what we've learned from Psalm 63?

You know, Psalm 78 reveals specific Jewish history, but it also reveals general human inclinations. The tendency to doubt God's ability to satisfy and to give into lesser cravings is, unfortunately, the most normal human thing ever. In fact, it can happen in life's "deserts" or even in life's "gardens." Think about it: In Genesis 3, we see Eve indulge a craving and a sneaking doubt that God could satisfy—not in a desert, but in a lush garden. Wherever we're standing, there's a strong pull to crave things that will not satisfy. Part of our work as Christ-followers is to protect our appetite for Him by putting to death lesser cravings and daily yielding our hunger pangs to Him, knowing that only He can satisfy.

So, it's time for some honest reflection. It's time to follow the lead of the writer of Psalm 78 (a guy named Asaph), and remember not just God's faithfulness, but our faithlessness:

Based on what you know is true, what is the source of true satisfaction? Use Psalm 63 as evidence.

What kinds of things do you reach for that ruin your appetite for God? What is the result of reaching for those things?

When you reach for those things, what true things are you not believing? (Read Ps. 78:22.)

Read Psalm 78:37 and write it below. Are you like the Israelites as they're described in this verse?

Read Psalm 63:3 and write it below. What is God like?

It's so good for us to pay attention to what God is like and to what we are like. It's painful, but only momentarily, because we know we are free right now to confess our sins and that God will be faithful to forgive them. Sister, as you take a hard look at yourself and all the cravings that desire to take hold of your heart, don't forget the gospel. God extended steadfast love to us through His Son Jesus, even though we didn't deserve it. He invites us to sit at His table and feast on what will truly satisfy, if only we'll put down the stale cookies and trust Him.

There is good news for the girl who craves: "The same God who created appetites in us has also created the means to their satisfaction."[4] Himself! Sister, the battle against cravings is lifelong and often brutal. When your spiritual stomach starts to growl, chew on this truth: "For *he* satisfies the longing soul, and the hungry soul *he* fills with good things" (Ps. 107:9, emphasis added).

CLOSING PRAYER

Write out a prayer of confession. You are safe to be honest with the Lord because He has already searched you and already knows you better than anyone else (Ps. 139:1). Tell Him what you crave and ask Him to satisfy. If you need help, borrow words from Psalm 63.

DEAR GOD,

_____

_____

_____

_____

_____

AMEN.

CLOSING RHYTHM

Read Psalm 63 or listen to it via an audio Bible or through one of the Psalm 63 songs we've discovered. Let it be a proclamation of truth and praise to battle against a world that would have you desire lesser things!

EAGERLY SEEKING GOD

PSALM 63

1 *O God, you are my God; earnestly I seek you;*

my soul thirsts for you;

my flesh faints for you,

as in a dry and weary land where there is no water.

2 *So I have looked upon you in the sanctuary,*

beholding your power and glory.

3 *Because your steadfast love is better than life,*

my lips will praise you.

4 *So I will bless you as long as I live;*

in your name I will lift up my hands.

5 *My soul will be satisfied as with fat and rich food, and my mouth*

will praise you with joyful lips,

6 *when I remember you upon my bed,*

and meditate on you in the watches of the night;

7 *for you have been my help,*

and in the shadow of your wings I will sing for joy.

8 *My soul clings to you;*

your right hand upholds me.

9 *But those who seek to destroy my life*

shall go down into the depths of the earth;

10 *they shall be given over to the power of the sword;*

they shall be a portion for jackals.

11 *But the king shall rejoice in God;*

all who swear by him shall exult,

for the mouths of liars will be stopped.

WATCH

Watch the video and fill in the blanks before transitioning to the Discuss section.

"… and meditate on you in the _____ of the _____." *Psalm 63:6*

How many military watches did the Jewish people have?

David seeks the _____ first.

Spoiler alert: _____ dies and _____ remains king. When David wrote this, he did not know that would be the _____ of the story.

DISCUSS

Read 2 Samuel 15:13-37 together, and then answer the questions.

DAVID'S LACK OF KNOWLEDGE ABOUT THE FUTURE

In 2 Samuel 15:13, a messenger says to David, "The hearts of the men of Israel have gone after Absalom." What does this mean? How did this happen?

Read 2 Samuel 15:19. Who is David talking about when he says "the king"? What does this reveal about David's worries?

DAVID'S PRAYER

READ 2 SAMUEL 15:31.

What does David pray for?

READ 2 SAMUEL 17:1-14.

Was David's prayer answered?

Do you think David knew this prayer was answered? Why or why not?

DAVID'S LONGING

READ VERSE 25.

In this tumultuous time, what does David long for?

What part of Psalm 63 does this remind you of?

BE CURIOUS

Is there anything else in the passage that stands out to you?

Imagine that you are in David's shoes. What would you be anxious about? What thoughts would fill your mind? What would you pray for?

SNEAK PEEK

If you have time and want to know how the story turns out (even though David didn't know what would happen), read 2 Samuel 18. If you don't have time, no worries—we'll get to it soon!

CLOSING PRAYER

DEAR GOD,

You are our God. Earnestly we seek You—in the morning and during the night. We know that despite the uncertain circumstances that surround us, You are our source of satisfaction. When everything seems shaky, help us remind ourselves and one another that You and Your character never change.

AMEN.

CLOSING RHYTHM

Saying Psalm 139 out loud during the night was a powerful habit for me when I was up late with my second child. With that in mind, read Psalm 63 out loud together.

DAY 1: OBSERVATION

...when I remember you upon my bed,
and meditate on you in the watches of the night

Do you ever get frustrated when someone says the same thing twice? I do—except that often, as soon as I recognize my frustration, I also realize that I wasn't paying attention the first time they said it. (Oops.)

Throughout history, communicators have used repetition to drive their point home. Repetition forces listeners to pay attention—especially if they were zoning out the first time—and it emphasizes the idea in the same way you'd emphasize a part in a book by underlining it. That's why the "R" in "DTR" is a crucial point in observation—we want to be sure we pay special attention to what the writer is emphasizing.

Often repetition isn't the same exact words being repeated, but synonyms of words being repeated. In other words, a teacher, writer, or speaker might say the same thing multiple times in different ways.

In poetry, repetition is often used to artfully emphasize and clarify an idea. In Hebrew poetry, like the Psalms, repetition is especially important. In fact, many Bible scholars have noted that Hebrew poetry "rhymes" ideas instead of words through a special kind of repetition called parallelism. One type of parallelism works like this: a thing is said the first time, and then it's said a second time but with more detail or drama. That's what we see here in verse 6. Draw arrows to connect the repeated parts:

...when I remember you upon my bed,
and meditate on you in the watches of the night

How is "watches of the night" more detailed and/or more dramatic than "bed"?

"Remember" and "meditate" repeat one another in the same way. Let's look into precisely why "meditate" is more detailed and/or more dramatic than "remember." Using an original language dictionary, look up both words:

Remember:

Meditate:

Okay, real talk: The definition for "meditate" is weird, isn't it?

Let's eavesdrop into a conversation between Tim and Jon on The Bible Project Podcast about this very thing. (I've highlighted the parts I want to you to pay special attention to.)

TIM: Rather than emptying your mind, this form of meditation is about filling your mind. But about filling your mind with something other than just your own thoughts. The word "meditate" in Hebrew is *hagah* and it occurs like eight or nine times. So it's not a super common word, but it's used enough. We have a very clear picture. Actually, the majority of the times that it's used, it's animals that do it.

JON: Oh, they're meditating? Interesting.

TIM: It describes what a bear does over its prey.

...

TIM: So what sound does a big bear make as it's eating an animal?

JON: Eating sounds.

TIM: It's like, "Harrh harrg."

JON: Oh, right.

TIM: Mouth noises, right?

JON: Right, yeah.

TIM: Like growling. The English word we have for that is growl.

JON: Growl, but also the smacking in the enjoyment.[1]

I am resisting describing the way my husband eats chocolate chip pancakes, but let's just say, "mouth noises," and leave it at that.

That's interesting, isn't it?

Zoom out a bit from verse 6 and write down David's full sentence (vv. 5-7) below. Then, circle anything that reminds you of this idea of "smacking in the enjoyment."

Just for fun, look up Psalm 34:8 and Psalm 34:10 and write both verses below.

What connections can you make between *hagah*, Psalm 34:8,10, and the spiritual hunger we talked about last week? Take a moment to piece the ideas together.

Okay, so *hagah*, or "meditate," implies some kind of enjoyable eating and noise. Flip back to the place where you wrote the definition for the word *meditate* and add in any new understanding you have. Then, write a brief definition of the word on your Psalm 63 text. When you've done these two things, check this box: ☐. Great job!

DEAR GOD,

You are my God. Thank You that in You, my soul can be satisfied as with fat and rich food. Thank You that I can remember You upon my bed and meditate on You in the watches of the night, when things seem especially dark and when I feel as if I'm in battle. Forgive me for all the times I haven't looked to You, and help me remember that I always can.

AMEN.

CLOSING RHYTHM

Read Psalm 63 out loud, say it with an audio Bible, or sing it along with one of the Psalm 63 songs we've discovered.

DAY 2: INTERPRETATION (SGC)

*...when I remember you upon my bed,
and meditate on you in the watches of the night*

We started out the week with more context (C), spent yesterday observing the text (O), and today we are going to dive into the third part of the recipe: interpretation (I). Before we get going, let's check in: Are you feeling better equipped for Bible study? If you felt compelled to study a book of the Bible, would you feel less intimidated to do so? Take some time to consider where you're at.

If you still feel overwhelmed, that's okay! Celebrate whatever progress has been made, and take heart that Bible study involves moments of difficulty for everyone—even pastors or men and women who've been trained for years! Here's a fun fact: the Latin root of the word "study" is "zeal,"[2] and zeal means "eagerness and ardent interest in pursuit of something."[3] The words "eagerness" and "ardent" here imply a warm enthusiasm—as in "I want to know this! I want to do this!" Who would've thought that the word "study" contains ingredients less like the stuff you'd find in a classroom and more like the stuff you'd find at a pep rally?

I am praying God will continue to increase your appetite, or zeal, for His Word as you study! Take a moment to ask God to increase your appetite. When you've done that, check this box: ☐

The way we've been learning to interpret the Bible is SGC, which stands for "super good coffee" or "silly goose Caroline" or (this is the real one) "Scripture, Gospel, Curiosity." Please imagine me saying this in a cheerleader voice like I'm leading you in a pep rally: "Ready? Okay!"

SCRIPTURE

CROSS-REFERENCES

- Look up Psalm 42:8 and write it below.

- How does this verse help you understand Psalm 63:6 better?

OTHER SCRIPTURE PASSAGES

Psalm 23:4 ← ——————————— Another psalm written by David!

- What location is mentioned in this text?

- In this location, where is God?

- Think about the words "even though." How is this a comfort?

Psalm 139:7-10 ←

- What locations are mentioned in this text?

Yet another psalm written by David!

- In every location, where is God?

- Think about the words "even there" in verse 10. How are these a comfort?

What connections can you make between all these Scripture passages and Psalm 63:6? How is it meaningful and helpful to remember that David wrote Psalm 23, Psalm 63, and Psalm 139?

GOSPEL

The gospel is the story of Jesus' perfect life, death, and resurrection, and the implications it has for us (sinners in need of saving) and the broken world in which we live.

How does the gospel help you more fully understand this part of Psalm 63?

If you're struggling to answer, consider this: How does the gospel offer light into dark places, the way meditating on God offers satisfaction to David in a dry place?

CURIOSITY

Is there any part of this verse you'd like to research more fully? Are there any lingering questions you have? Take the time to chase after them. It's okay if you don't arrive at any answers!

CLOSING PRAYER

DEAR GOD,

You are my God. Earnestly I seek You. My soul will be satisfied as with fat and rich food, and my mouth will praise You with joyful lips, when I remember You upon my bed, and meditate on You in the watches of the night. Increase my hunger for Your Word! Make me zealous in my study!

AMEN.

CLOSING RHYTHM

Read Psalm 63 out loud, say it with an audio Bible, or sing it along with one of the Psalm 63 songs we've discovered.

DAY 3: APPLICATION

...when I remember you upon my bed,
and meditate on you in the watches of the night

Hebrews 4:12 says, "For the word of God is living and active, sharper than any two-edged sword, piercing to the division of soul and of spirit, of joints and of marrow, and discerning the thoughts and intentions of the heart." When you read the Bible, God's Word and God's Spirit partner with you to discern your thoughts and your heart's intentions—the stuff no one else can see. This kind of exposure is intimate and important because, when we are faithful to obey what is revealed, we are made to look more like Christ, even in the unseen places.

Why am I telling you this? Because I don't want you to rely on outside sources for application. Though Bible studies, pastors, teachers, parents, and friends are a great tool to help us apply the Bible, nothing compares to the work the Holy Spirit does as you read the Bible for yourself. Only God's Word and God's Spirit can get all the way down into those unseen places and truly discern our insides and bring change. God has given you everything you need to pursue Christlikeness: His Word and His Spirit.

> So, before I tell you how I think we can apply this passage, prayerfully answer the application question for yourself: "How should this change the way I think and live?" (If it helps, cover up the rest of today's study with a piece of paper while you think it over.)

Here's what I think: Verse 6 is a much-needed help for those of us whose nights are often filled with anxiety, fear, and overwhelming feelings: Remember God. Remember His Word.

This glimpse into David's nighttime habit of meditating on the Lord is part of a sentence that's all about satisfaction. The meditating brings about satisfaction for him, even during the vulnerable hours of night watches, and meditating on the Lord can do the same for us.

> Look up Isaiah 26:3 and write it below:

> What is the result of a mind that is fixed on God?

> Why might fixing our minds on God bring peace (like it says in Isa. 26:3) and satisfaction (like it says in Ps. 63:5-6)?

You know that feeling when you realize you're sitting in a seat that wasn't intended for you? Maybe you grabbed another person's seat at a restaurant or you didn't realize there was a seating chart in class. Whatever the situation, there's something unsettling about sitting in the wrong seat.

Sister, often our minds aren't sitting in the right seat. We pull up a pile of anxiety and sit there. We pull up a pile of terrifying stories and possibilities and sit there. All the while, there are true, solid things about God that we can rest our minds upon. And oh, the deliciousness, satisfaction, and peace that results from a mind that is sitting in the right place! As Tim Keller says, "Training our hearts to spend our sleepless night in praise and fellowship with God will redeem our frustration, turning it into cherished intimacy with our Savior."[4]

So practically, how do we do that? Well, we have to fill our minds with truth—which is exactly what you're doing through this deep-dive into Psalm 63—and then we have to discipline our wandering minds to stay in their seat.

What kinds of thoughts plague you at night?

What true things about God or what verses or passages in the Bible might help you battle those thoughts?

What are some practical things you can do to discipline your mind to stay in its proper seat?

DAY 4: MEMORIZATION

*...when I remember you upon my bed,
and meditate on you in the watches of the night*

Remember eavesdropping on that conversation between Tim and Jon? Because the Hebrew word for meditation, *hagah*, involves not just enjoyable eating but also noises, Tim and Jon go on to discuss a helpful application for this concept—reading the Bible out loud instead of silently. Tim says, "It engages my whole body and mind in a way that's very different from when I read silently ... when you read it aloud all the time, you also begin to think about it all the time. It's what fills your mind."[5]

Perhaps David was literally saying God's Word out loud during the night watches in the wilderness. I know that's what I was doing in the nursery in the middle of the night, and I experienced tremendous comfort and delight as a result. *Hagah* isn't a "make everything better" pill, but orally proclaiming truth is certainly a powerful practice!

Can you think of ways it might benefit you, especially in the dark times?

Here's something to think about: When I was in that dark nursery and rocking a crying baby, it wasn't possible for me to have an open copy of the Bible in front of me. Even holding a phone was a little challenging. David likely didn't have a copy of the text in front of him either. Instead, God's Word has to be stored away where we can access it at any time: in our hearts. Memorization is immensely powerful because it forces a person to truly meditate, or *hagah*, on the text. Genuinely, it changed my life to habitually speak God's Word from memory out loud.

Look up the following verses:

- **Psalm 1:1-2**

- **Psalm 119:13-16**

- **Psalm 119:48**

- **Psalm 119:62**

What do these verses teach you about the value of meditating on and memorizing God's Word?

Your job today is to come up with a memorization plan for Psalm 63. Because we are six weeks into the study, you are already pretty familiar with at least verses 1-6, but we want to take the next step and intentionally pack the full Psalm into your heart so that you can access it in any of life's wildernesses and feast on God's truth.

Before we create the plan, I want to remind you of a foundational idea I shared with you at the very beginning of the study: delight is always propped up by structure. Remember the roller coaster metaphor? Roller coasters would be death traps if they weren't carefully and thoughtfully constructed. But because of their careful structure, we are able to experience lots of delight! Because I carefully stored Psalm 139 in my mind, I was able to experience a lot of delight in a dark place—and I am still experiencing delight because I find myself meditating on that passage all the time. As your sister in Christ, I want this for you, too. I don't want you to be the one watching the roller coaster and thinking, "It'd be great to do that"—I want to see your hands in the air and delight on your face. So, let's make a plan.

MY MEMORIZATION PLAN
GOAL: MEMORIZE PSALM 63 (11 VERSES)

1. Create a schedule. If you want to have Psalm 63 memorized by the time this study is over, you can memorize 3-4 verses a week from now until the remainder of the study. If you need more time, take it! Do whatever is your best bet for storing the passage away. This is an investment in your future wilderness self. Use the space below to decide what verses you'll memorize when.

Sample Schedule:

WEEK 1	WEEK 2	WEEK 3
verses 1-4	verses 5-8	verses 9-11

2. Based on your unique schedule and availability, decide when and where you'll work on it:

   Memorization Tip: Cramming doesn't work. The brain loves small, repeated increments[6], so grab routine chunks of time daily to work on it (i.e., on the way to school, while doing makeup, and so on).

3. Based on your unique learning style and interests, decide how you'll work on it:

   Memorization Tip: Consider how you learn. Are you a kinetic learner (connected to movement)? Work on memorization while exercising or make up motions. An auditory learner? Listen to the passage on the Bible app until you can say it along with the speaker. A visual learner? Write or type out the chunk you're working on over and over again in a visually memorable way (like putting important words larger and in a different font). Other ideas: Research apps that might help, like the Bible Memory app, and ask women in your church how they memorize Scripture. Maybe someone has a method that will really click for you!

4. Decide who will keep you accountable. Then, reach out to them today and ask them to check in with you!

   Memorization Tip: Scientist Jon Medina noticed that his "eagerness to yap about the experience provided the key ingredient" for something to stick in his long term memory. In other words: Find someone you can chat about the text with![7]

   When you feel that you've created a plan that is manageable for your life, check this box: ☐. Way to go!

   Even armed with a great plan, it can be difficult to follow through. What can you tell yourself when you feel overwhelmed, annoyed, or too lazy to follow through?

You know what? It's always helpful to memorize something you're already studying, because we best remember things that mean something to us, things that don't seem random but have an order we understand. So as you memorize, continue to participate in this study wholeheartedly, fight for meaning, and seek to get a grasp of the beginning, middle, and end of the passage.

Even still, trust me on this: If you block out every word I've shared in this study but diligently memorize Psalm 63, you are coming away with the greater treasure. There's nothing I can offer you that's better than the Word of God living in your heart. May this passage provide for you a solid foundation for delight and peace even in life's wildernesses!

CLOSING PRAYER

DEAR GOD,

You are my God. Earnestly I seek You. Satisfy my soul, as my mouth praises You and as I meditate on You in the watches of the night. I believe Your steadfast love is better than life—strengthen me to store Your words in my heart that I might not forget what is true.

AMEN.

CLOSING RHYTHM

Read Psalm 63 out loud. Hagah!

BUCKETS OF DELIGHT

PSALM 63

1 *O God, you are my God; earnestly I seek you;*

my soul thirsts for you;

my flesh faints for you,

as in a dry and weary land where there is no water.

2 *So I have looked upon you in the sanctuary,*

beholding your power and glory.

3 *Because your steadfast love is better than life,*

my lips will praise you.

4 *So I will bless you as long as I live;*

in your name I will lift up my hands.

5 *My soul will be satisfied as with fat and rich food, and my mouth*

will praise you with joyful lips,

6 *when I remember you upon my bed,*

and meditate on you in the watches of the night;

7 *for you have been my help,*

and in the shadow of your wings I will sing for joy.

8 *My soul clings to you;*

your right hand upholds me.

9 *But those who seek to destroy my life*

shall go down into the depths of the earth;

10 *they shall be given over to the power of the sword;*

they shall be a portion for jackals.

11 *But the king shall rejoice in God;*

all who swear by him shall exult,

for the mouths of liars will be stopped.

WATCH

Watch the video and fill up your theme buckets together. Then, consider your observations before moving on to the Discuss section.

We are going to observe Psalm 63 by using the tool of _____.

"For you have been my help, and in the _____ of your _____ I will _____ for_____." Psalm 63:7

THEME BUCKETS

"for you have been my help,
and in the shadow of your wings I will sing for joy.
My soul clings to you;
your right hand upholds me."

Darkness (shadow)	Body parts (wings, hand)
Observations/Connections:	**Observations/Connections:**

Praise (sing for joy)	Soul

Observations/Connections:	Observations/Connections:

DISCUSS

What connections do you see within each theme?

Do you notice any connections between the themes? For example, is there a connection between "praise" and "soul"?

Is there a theme that is particularly interesting to you or catches your attention? What is it? Why does it grab you?

Does this "theme bucket" strategy make sense to you? Do you think you could do it yourself for another passage if you needed to?

CLOSING PRAYER

DEAR GOD,

You are our God. Earnestly we seek You. Our souls thirst for You, and we know that You are the only One who can satisfy. Fill us up with Your Word, and make us hungry to know You more.

AMEN.

CLOSING RHYTHM

Read Psalm 63 out loud together. Remember, this Psalm was not just written for David's personal worship—it was purposefully included in the nation of Israel's songbook for the purpose of corporate worship. The original audience would have sung this out loud together!

DAY 1: CONTEXT + OBSERVATION

*...for you have been my help, and in the shadow of your wings I will
sing for joy. My soul clings to you; your right hand upholds me.*

CONTEXT

As we continue studying Psalm 63:7-8, let's remind ourselves of a bit of context we may have
overlooked or forgotten.

**Read 1 Samuel 16:7-13,18-23, and write down what these verses reveal about
God and about David.**

God	David

**Now read 1 Samuel 17:37-49. Write down what this passage reveals about God
and about David.**

God	David

These familiar stories are the first time David is mentioned in the Bible. David was an unlikely
candidate for king, yet God selected him. David was an unlikely candidate to overtake a mighty
and fearsome warrior, yet God empowered him to do just that. I suspect the experiences were
foundational in David's life and informed the way he lived. My favorite part of the passage
is 1 Samuel 16:13, which says, "And the Spirit of the LORD rushed up on David from that day
forward." Wow!

OBSERVATION

With that in mind, let's observe Psalm 63 by DTR-ing the text. In this week's group session,
we spent a lot of time on T (themes), so today, we'll focus our energies on D (definitions) and
R (repetition).

D (DEFINITIONS)

Look up the following words in an original language dictionary and write down the best definition. If you need further clarification, look up the word in an English language dictionary. Then, write a summary of the definition over each word in your Psalm 63 text.

help:

sing for joy:

clings:

upholds:

R (REPETITION)

Remember that repetition is a repeated word or phrase. Last week we talked about an interesting kind of repetition we see in the Hebrew poetry, parallelism, in which ideas are "rhymed" instead of words. We see a similar structure here, but the "rhyme" scheme is a bit different. It's what fancy people would call chiastic structure, and what I, an unfancy person, would call an idea sandwich. This means the ideas "rhyme" or are repeated sandwich-style, with a "rhyme" scheme of ABBA. Take a look at verses 7-8, and fill in the rhyme scheme as best you can by summarizing each part of the verse:

The Lord _____ (v. 7a)

David _____ (v. 7b)

David _____ (v. 8a)

The Lord _____ (v. 8b)

Let's be unfancy and think of it as an idea sandwich. What connections can you make about the two slices of bread?

What connections can you make about the stuff that's inside the bread?

Just as David experienced in his early years, God makes the first move. God is his helper, so David responds by rejoicing in the safe place God created for him. There, David responds again by following close, and God continues to be God—holding on to David. This pair of verses functions like a warm embrace: God holding on to David, and David holding right back. Now that is a delicious sandwich.

DEAR GOD,

You are my God. Therefore, I earnestly seek You right back, just like David did. You are my helper, and I will sing for joy in the shadow of Your wings. My soul will cling to You as Your right hand upholds me. Thank You for Your steadfast love.

AMEN.

CLOSING RHYTHM

Read Psalm 63 out loud, say it with an audio Bible, or sing it along with one of the Psalm 63 songs we've discovered.

DAY 2: INTERPRETATION (SGC)

...for you have been my help, and in the shadow of your wings I will sing for joy. My soul clings to you; your right hand upholds me.

Yesterday we revisited the context (C) and observed the text (O), so you know what's next— Interpretation. Our tools for interpretation are SGC, which stands for "sad giraffes cry" (it's true), or "Scripture, Gospel, Curiosity."

SCRIPTURE

I used a study Bible[1] to find the cross-references mentioned in today's study, and then to find other times in Scripture when the same word is noted, I used the free online concordance (Blue Letter Bible) that automatically comes up when I looked up the word's definition.

Are you comfortable doing these two things on your own? Write down how you think you'll do.

If you're unsure, you may want to ask for help or spend some time figuring it out on your own. Now that I know how to use these tools, it hardly takes any time at all to gather the information I want, and that is a huge benefit to my study.

You'll notice on the list below that some of the places have a blank instead of a verse. These are ones you should complete on your own. Write all the verses out or jot down their key phrases. If any of these verses are particularly helpful for you as you seek to understand Psalm 63:7-8, you may want to write their reference or part of the verse on your Psalm 63 text. When you have done all of this, check the box: ☐. Wahoo!

HELP/"EZRAH"

Cross-references	Other times "ezrah" is used
none	_____
	_____

SHADOW/"TSEL"

Cross-references	Other times "tsel" is used
_____	Psalm 36:7
	Psalm 57:1

CLINGS/"DABAQ"

Cross-references	Other times "dabaq" is used
_____	Ruth 1:14
	2 Kings 18:6

UPHOLDS/"TAMAK"

Cross-references	Other times "dabaq" is used
Psalm 41:12	Exodus 17:12
	Isaiah 41:10

GOSPEL

I know that was a lot of work! Thank you for your perseverance. I hope you were able to uncover the depth and nuance of these terms. Because you've worked so hard, I want to mostly plate up this next part for you. The second way we can interpret Scripture is with the gospel. Remember that even though David had no idea God would send His Son, Jesus, in human form to pay the penalty for sin, all of his writings still point to Jesus. This is one of the things that makes Bible study a wonderful and endlessly fascinating puzzle! Here's how I see the gospel at work in Psalm 63:7-8:

"HELP"

David calls God His help, and because of Jesus' perfect life, death, and resurrection, we are able to see another way that God shows up as a helper. Look up John 14:26. This verse is wedged in the middle of Jesus comforting His disciples before He dies.

Who is "the helper"? Why is this news a comfort?

"SHADOW OF YOUR WINGS"

If you remember from our observation during the group session, "shadow" is one of several references to literal or spiritual darkness. However, "shadow of your wings" is a safe darkness, a refuge that God's metaphorical body ("wings") offers to David. It shields him from the other kinds of darkness, like the kind his enemies will one day endure (vv. 9-10). Because of Jesus' perfect life, death, and resurrection, Christians can say this same thing. Jesus' body, broken for all sinners, is a refuge for those who follow Him, protecting them from "going down into the depths of the earth" (v. 9) and being "given over to the power of the sword" (v. 10). All of humanity deserves death and destruction, but because Jesus paid the penalty and surrendered His body, Christians find safety in the shadow of His wings.

Do you see any other gospel connections in Psalm 63:7-8?

CURIOSITY

Is there anything else you're curious about in this passage? Take some time to collect your questions or jot down points of confusion and use the tools you have to chase down more clarity.

CLOSING PRAYER

DEAR GOD,

You are my God. Earnestly I seek You—thank You that I can seek You through Your Word. You are my help! In the shadow of Your wings, I will sing for joy. Give me wisdom to understand the full significance of this precious gift.

AMEN

CLOSING RHYTHM

Read Psalm 63 out loud, say it with an audio Bible, or sing it along with one of the Psalm 63 songs we've discovered.

DAY 3: APPLICATION

...for you have been my help, and in the shadow of your wings I will sing for joy. My soul clings to you; your right hand upholds me.

The final part of the recipe is Application (A). Just for review, fill in the recipe as best you can:

_____ (5Ws & H)

_____ (_____)

_____ (SGC)

_____

Magnifique! [Insert chef's kiss.] You are a genius. As we've studied, you may have already begun to develop some ideas about how this part of Psalm 63 can be applied.

If you have any thoughts about how verses 7-8 should change the way we think or live, write them below.

As we begin to consider how we can apply this text, let's look back at that idea sandwich because it so clearly outlines the four actions present in this verse:

The Lord helps (v. 7a)

David sings (v. 7b)

David clings (v. 8a)

The Lord upholds (v. 8b)

Who acts first? What is David's response?

This part of the text reveals two things God does. Do you believe God does these things? Have you experienced them?

This part of the text also reveals two things David does. Do you find yourself doing these things? If not, why? What is the disconnect?

In your current circumstances, what might it look like to sing and to cling to God?

We've been using the ESV translation of the Bible in this study, but often using multiple translations can help us get a better grasp of the content. For example, the CSB translation says for verse 8, "I follow close to you; your right hand holds on to me." In other words, "clinging" means "following close."

As David clings to God, what does God do?

As you cling to God, what can you be sure God will do?

This verse reveals the beautiful dynamics of a relationship with God—He initiates it and sustains it, while we praise Him and follow close.

Which part of the relationship presents the most hesitation for you—holding on to Him or knowing that He holds on to you?

CLOSING PRAYER

Based on what you've discovered in today's session, write an honest prayer to the Lord. Do you need to praise Him for being your help and for upholding you? Do you need to confess your failure to sing? Do you need wisdom to better grasp who God is and what He's done so that you can sing (Jas. 1:5-8)? Do you need to confess your failure to cling? Do you need wisdom to know practically how to cling (Jas. 1:5-8)? Pour out your heart before Him.

Trust in him at all times, O people; pour out your heart before him; God is a refuge for us. **PSALM 62:8**

DEAR GOD,

_____

_____

_____

AMEN.

Read Psalm 63 out loud, say it with an audio Bible, or sing it along with one of the Psalm 63 songs we've discovered.

DAY 4: BE A PSALMIST

...for you have been my help, and in the shadow of your wings I will sing for joy. My soul clings to you; your right hand upholds me.

Take a moment to remember what we've learned this week. Is there anything you've intended to jot down on your Psalm 63 text but haven't? Take a moment to do that—it will help you remember what you've learned! When you've done it, check this box: ☐. Yay!

Have you ever heard someone say, "I'm a word person"? Word people are nerds like me who perk up in English class, delight in freshly sharpened pencils, sometimes find themselves drooling in the journal aisle at Target, and may or may not love the smell of books.

Are you a word person? Are you a numbers person? Are you a lunch-is-the-best-part-of-school person?

God is a word person. (He's a numbers person, too, and possibly a lunch person, but that's not the point today.) Why? Because language is foundational to His relationship with humanity. After all, in Genesis 1, we see God creating the world by speaking words. This is one important way that God reveals Himself to His people—through creation. Then, in John 1, we see Jesus presented as the Word. This is another important way God reveals Himself to His people—through His Son taking on human flesh. Finally, we can catch a glimpse of our own Bibles and realize it's jam-packed with—you guessed it—words. This is yet another important way God reveals Himself to His people—through the biblical record. Bottom line: words matter. Words matter to God, and words are an essential way He reaches out to us.

One thrilling thing about the psalms is that they contain words that humans spoke back to God. These prayers and songs stirred in the hearts of real people with significant struggles, strong emotions, and big questions. This is good news for us, because chances are we, too, have significant struggles, strong emotions, and big questions, and the psalms meet us right where we are. As Nancy Guthrie says, "The psalms provide us with a vocabulary for expressing the broad range of human emotions—even, or perhaps especially, the negative ones—to God in a way that draws us

God Reveals Himself To His People Through the Bible.

toward him rather than estranging us from him. They coach us in worship that is both pleasing to him and beneficial to us, which includes expressing both our gladness and our sadness."[2]

What a gift the psalms are! Any time we don't know what to pray, we can borrow a psalm. Any time we experience an emotion that feels too confusing to articulate, we can borrow a psalm. Any time we don't know what to say to a friend, we can borrow a psalm. The psalms teach us how to express ourselves.

CLOSING PRAYER

Today I want you to model the psalms by offering some of your words to God. Our words are never a substitute for the Bible, but writing can be such a powerful way for us to consider who God is and to reflect on what is going on in our hearts and minds. These words can be honest and display whatever emotion you discover in your heart, and you are free to borrow whatever you wish from the psalms themselves. If this activity feels too vague, here are some ideas you might consider:

- *Choose a characteristic of God you've encountered recently and praise Him for it.*
- *Borrow one of the themes we gathered in our buckets during the group session and craft a psalm around that theme.*
- *Borrow the structure of Psalm 63 and shape it to fit your current state of heart and mind.*
- *Pick a few of your favorite psalms and stitch pieces of them together to accurately reflect your emotions and questions.*

_____

_____

_____

_____

_____

_____

What did crafting this "psalm" reveal about yourself? What did it reveal about your relationship with God?

CLOSING RHYTHM

Read Psalm 63 out loud, say it with an audio Bible, or sing it along with one of the Psalm 63 songs we've discovered.

WHAT ABOUT THE WEIRD STUFF IN THE BIBLE?

PSALM 63

1 *O God, you are my God; earnestly I seek you;*

my soul thirsts for you;

my flesh faints for you,

as in a dry and weary land where there is no water.

2 *So I have looked upon you in the sanctuary,*

beholding your power and glory.

3 *Because your steadfast love is better than life,*

my lips will praise you.

4 *So I will bless you as long as I live;*

in your name I will lift up my hands.

5 *My soul will be satisfied as with fat and rich food, and my mouth*

will praise you with joyful lips,

6 *when I remember you upon my bed,*

and meditate on you in the watches of the night;

7 *for you have been my help,*

and in the shadow of your wings I will sing for joy.

8 *My soul clings to you;*

your right hand upholds me.

9 *But those who seek to destroy my life*

shall go down into the depths of the earth;

10 *they shall be given over to the power of the sword;*

they shall be a portion for jackals.

11 *But the king shall rejoice in God;*

all who swear by him shall exult,

for the mouths of liars will be stopped.

WATCH

Watch the video and fill in the blanks before transitioning to the Discuss section.

We always want to interpret the Bible with _____.

Our tools for interpretation are S_____ , G_____ , and C_____ .

The gospel is the story of Jesus' life, death, and _____.

According to Ephesians 6:12, the gospel changes who the _____ is.

In the _____ covenant, we are the enemy.

The enemy is _____ and the enemy is our own _____.

DISCUSS

In general, what do you do when you feel awkward or uncomfortable?

Have you read anything in the Bible that made you feel uncomfortable?

What do we do with the weird parts of the Bible?

Think about our recipe. Is there a particular part of the recipe that might be extra helpful when it comes to the weird stuff?

READ MATTHEW 5:17-48.

The people listening when Jesus said all of this had been raised under the teaching of the Old Testament and had no idea that Jesus would die on the cross and be raised again.

How might these words have shocked the original hearers?

Based on this passage, what is Jesus' overall message?

READ ROMANS 5:10.

Who was once the enemy?

READ EPHESIANS 6:12.

Who is the new enemy?

What is the difference between the old covenant and the new covenant? Why is all of this old versus new stuff important when we're interpreting the Bible?

Look at Psalm 63:9-10. Under the old covenant, who is "those"/"they"? Under the new covenant, who is "those"/"they"?

CLOSING PRAYER

DEAR GOD,

You are our God. Earnestly we seek You. Give us eyes to see our true enemy: the sin that threatens our hearts and Satan who desires to overthrow Your kingdom. We ask that those who seek to destroy our lives would go down into the depths of the earth. They will be given over to the power of the sword. Thank You for inviting us to be Your family even though we were enemies. Thank You that we can have confidence Your kingdom will prevail.

AMEN.

CLOSING RHYTHM

Read Psalm 63 out loud together. Remember, this Psalm was not just written for David's personal worship—it was purposefully included in the nation of Israel's songbook for the purpose of corporate worship. The original audience would have sung this out loud together!

DAY 1: CONTEXT

But those who seek to destroy my life shall go down into the depths of the earth; they shall be given over to the power of the sword; they shall be a portion for jackals.

In our group time yesterday, we interpreted "those" and "they" in verses 9 and 10 by holding them up against the gospel. As a refresher, answer the questions below.

In the Old Covenant, who is the those or they?

In the New Covenant, who is the those or they?

In Psalm 63:9-10, David declares the fate of his enemies. Let's take a look at how the story ends to see if David's proclamations over the original "those"/"they" are accurate. Read 2 Samuel 18, and when you're done, check this box: ☐

Briefly list the events of 2 Samuel 18.

Does anything seem startling? Place an asterisk by anything that makes you raise your eyebrows. Did you uncover any information you'd like to add to your context notes? If so, take the time to add it.

Based on the narrative, does it seem as if David's Psalm 63 proclamations ("down into the depths of the earth," "given over to the power of the sword," "shall be a portion for jackals") are accurate?

What is David's response to Absalom's death? Does this make sense? Why or why not?

Can you get a sense of David's broken heart and his conflicted desires? What a tragic scenario it is when family becomes enemies! Remember during our group session, we marveled over the truth of the gospel, which is the opposite of this story: when enemies become family.

David's family has much to teach us about God's family, and David's son Absalom has much to teach us about God's Son, Jesus. Let's spend the rest of our time today comparing these two men. Why? Two reasons:

1. Smart Bible people have long acknowledged something called "the three offices of Christ"[1]—demonstrating how Jesus Christ was the perfect prophet, priest, and king. We see examples throughout the Bible of prophets, priests, and kings who offer shadowy glimpses of the full glory that was to come in Christ. (For example, in Acts 3:22, Peter shares Moses' words from Deuteronomy 18:15 to reveal how Moses, a prophet, was a shadow of the fullness that was to come in Christ.) Considering these three offices is useful because it helps us see Christ over the entirety of the Bible, and the "shadows" give us a better grasp of Christ's fullness.

2. One of the best ways to remember that God's steadfast love is better than life is to hold what God offers up against what the world offers. None of these "shadows" will fully satisfy, and they certainly can't save—but they point to the One who will.

Absalom	Jesus
Son of David	_____ (Matt. 1:1; 9:27; 21:9)
Without blemish (2 Sam. 14:25)	_____ (1 Peter 1:9)
Beloved by his father (_____)	_____ (Matt. 3:17)
Death by hanging from a tree (_____)	_____ (Acts 5:30)
Rebellion/death breaks family	Perfect life/death/resurrection _____ (Rom. 8:16)

To close, write 2 Samuel 7:12-13 below:

God made this promise to David long before Absalom's rebellion. Did God keep His promise? How?

CLOSING PRAYER

DEAR GOD,

You are my God. Earnestly I seek You. Thank You that I can know You through Your Word, that we can see clues of the good news of the gospel on every page of the Bible! Your steadfast love really is better than life.

AMEN.

CLOSING RHYTHM

Read Psalm 63 out loud, say it with an audio Bible, or sing it along with one of the Psalm 63 songs we've discovered.

DAY 2: OBSERVATION

But those who seek to destroy my life shall go down into the depths of the earth; they shall be given over to the power of the sword; they shall be a portion for jackals.

Here's a very churchy scenario I may have found myself in a time or two: I'm laughing and joking with someone, we're having a great time, and out of nowhere, they stop smiling and say very solemnly, "But you know, God is so good." I mean, of course He's good, but why we gotta get so serious so fast? Can't we say that same thing without suddenly cannon-balling into the serious side of the pool? I have whiplash from that tone shift!

That's what we're experiencing in Psalm 63 when we get to verse 9: a tone shift. Did it give you whiplash?

Here's what I've come to realize about sudden tone shifts in the psalms. It's not about the writer having a sudden change in mood or emotion. (Remember, the psalms aren't ripped out pages from someone's diary but carefully planned songs that were thoughtfully included in the nation's hymnbook.) Instead, it's often about the writer sharing the "flip side" of the concept explored in the rest of the psalm. For example, in Psalm 63, we see David heaping praise upon God for His steadfast love. What we see in verses 9-10 is the opposite of the security God's followers find in Him: the shaky fate of those who stand against God and His followers.

Remember that our observation tools are DTR—Definitions, Themes, and Repetition. Last week we collected themes in buckets, and I want us to do this for one particular theme I've noticed throughout Psalm 63—feasting.

Take a moment to fill up a theme bucket with everything you can find about eating, feasting, and other related ideas—and don't forget to include the "flip side" of feasting.

While David expresses both the hunger and satisfaction he finds in the Lord, those who oppose David don't feast at all—in fact, they are feasted upon. Yikes!

Hold verses 9-10 up against the rest of the psalm. What other "flip side" moments can you collect?

The Bible is full of these tension points. After all, the good news of the gospel is a "flip side" moment in itself: the horror of our sin and the fearsome holiness of God held up against the magnitude of God's grace through Jesus' death on the cross.

> Why is it important that we observe all the different "tones" in the Bible? How might we undermine God's intended message if we only paid attention to the pretty, quotable parts of the Bible and of this psalm?

> How might we undermine God's intended message if we only paid attention to the pretty parts of the gospel story?

To wrap up today, take a moment to remember the Bible reading recipe by filling in the blanks below. It's my hope and prayer that God will use this recipe to give you courage and equip you to dive into even the most confusing waters of Scripture!

_____ is for _____ (5Ws & H)

_____ is for _____ (____ ____ ____)

_____ is for _____ (____ ____ ____)

_____ is for _____

And look—I can't let you go without reminding you of a really important truth. If you are a Christ follower, Jesus didn't simply save you from your sin—He saved you to a family. As you navigate confusing parts of the Bible, don't forget to ask your family for help! Who is following Jesus a few steps ahead of you who could be a helpful resource for you as you earnestly seek God?

CLOSING PRAYER

DEAR GOD,

You are my God. Earnestly I seek You. Give me courage to seek You and seek Your wisdom even in parts of Scripture that confuse and concern me. Show me who else is seeking You and how I can seek You alongside them.

AMEN.

CLOSING RHYTHM

Read Psalm 63 out loud, say it with an audio Bible, or sing it along with one of the Psalm 63 songs we've discovered.

DAY 3: INTERPRETATION + APPLICATION

But those who seek to destroy my life shall go down into the depths of the earth; they shall be given over to the power of the sword; they shall be a portion for jackals.

Confession: I have been laughing about the word "jackals" since I started brainstorming this study. We're disconnected from this fox-like animal in our modern lives, so it feels decidedly random to find them mentioned in a beloved psalm. The word glares at us from the pages: JACKALS. It sounds like an ineffective insult we'd yell ("Yeah, well you're a jackal!"), and then feel really embarrassed ("Ugh, I can't believe I called her a jackal and now I can never show my face at school again."). If you were reading this Psalm out loud at church, "jackals" is the part that would throw off the vibe of the Psalm with such splendid awkwardness.

INTERPRETATION (SGC)

Admittedly, I've been intrigued by jackals in an unspiritual way, but intrigued nonetheless. I've found that an inquisitive mind is good for my faith, as long as I use it with integrity and keep the whole of the text in mind. This is that third part of interpretation: C, for curiosity. (If you recall, we've already done quite a bit of S and G in our group session this week!) Curiosity simply means "interest leading to inquiry."[2] It means paying attention to what grabs your attention and deciding to find out more.

My curiosity demanded I know more about jackals—especially because I don't want to be the kind of person who side-steps the awkward parts of the Bible. So, I did what any inquisitive, responsible Bible scholar would do while interpreting the Bible: I watched jackal YouTube videos.

As I watched the jackal videos, I was struck by this: Those are some sneaky dudes. In the first video I saw, a jackal schemed his way into devouring a baby seal.[3] (Yes, a baby seal, the cutest animal that has ever existed, became a portion for jackals.) I also discovered in my searching that jackals have long been associated with death because they're often found lurking around cemeteries in hopes of feasting on a dead body.[4] In fact, in all the other places in Scripture where the word for "jackal" is found, it's associated with death and despair.[5]

So while the rest of the Psalm speaks of life and feasting, verse 10 implies death and feasting. When David says, "they will become a meal for jackals," he is saying his enemies will come to a tragic, undignified end. With all that has been done throughout history to honor and protect the bodies of the deceased, it's not difficult to see how a jackal is capable of destroying dignity and exacerbating the pain of death.

APPLICATION

As we seek to apply verses 9-10 to our lives, let's map out what David is saying.

List the things David says await his enemies:

If you remember from our group session, we cannot simply apply David's words to the people on earth whom we consider our enemies. Why not?

Who is your true enemy? (Hint: Remember Eph. 6:12.)

Based on Psalm 63:9-10, what is the inevitable end to that enemy?

How do these verses about death and destruction offer us hope because of the gospel?

With all of this in mind, how can we apply verses 9-10 responsibly? In other words, how should this part of the text change the way we think and live?

CLOSING PRAYER

DEAR GOD,

You are my God. Earnestly I seek You. I know Your steadfast love is better than life! I know that sin and the enemy who seeks to destroy my life shall go down into the depths of the earth, shall be given over to the power of the sword, shall be a portion for jackals. Thank You for the ultimate victory I find in You. Until that day, I cling to You, and Your right hand upholds me.

AMEN.

CLOSING RHYTHM

Read Psalm 63 out loud, say it with an audio Bible, or sing it along with one of the Psalm 63 songs we've discovered.

tools for interpretation:

☑ SCRIPTURE

☑ GOSPEL

☑ CURIOSITY

DAY 4: MEMORIZATION

But those who seek to destroy my life shall go down into the depths of the earth; they shall be given over to the power of the sword; they shall be a portion for jackals.

Since we've been wading through weird parts of Scripture this week, let's do it one more time. Read Ezekiel 3:1-3 below and circle anything that stands out to you. Underline anything that reminds you of Psalm 63.

And he said to me, 'Son of man, eat whatever you find here. Eat this scroll, and go, speak to the house of Israel.' So I opened my mouth, and he gave me this scroll to eat. And he said to me, 'Son of man, feed your belly with this scroll that I give you and fill your stomach with it.' Then I ate it, and it was in my mouth as sweet as honey. **EZEKIEL 3:1-3**

Ezekiel literally ate a scroll (God's Word), and it was literally delicious! How about that? I think you can see where I'm going. Forks up.

When I was in my early 20s, I heard a new Chick-fil-A® was opening nearby, and I learned that anyone who camped out on site the day of the opening would win free Chick-fil-A for a year. My taste buds tap-danced at the thought of it, and my wallet said, "This would help." I hopped in the car, and on the way, I brainstormed ways to get out of work. Unfortunately, by the time I arrived, it was clear that my place of employment was not going to support my need for ongoing free chicken sandwiches (rude!), so I waved to the cows and headed back home. Being an adult is so lame.

Why am I telling this uneventful story with a terrible ending? Though camping out at Chick-fil-A had a cost of time and discomfort, I was willing to do it because the treasure was something I believed had value and deliciousness. Memorizing Scripture is a similar thing—it costs us time and discomfort, but if we understand the value and deliciousness of the treasure before us, we're willing to pay the cost.

Now here's the thing: If you're truly convinced in your heart and not just your head that memorizing God's Word is a yummy treasure, you probably want to, and thus you're probably getting it done. But if your "want to" is broken, we have to rev up our plan, eat the scroll anyway, and push through until the "want to" catches up. In my experience, we don't truly grasp how yummy and valuable memorization is until we've done it! (I supposed I'd never have considered camping out at Chick-fil-A if I hadn't already tasted my fair share of chicken sandwiches.)

So, let's reflect and then revitalize:

REFLECT

Flip back to your Memorization Plan on page 96, and then consider:

- How is the memorization going?
- Is there a particular part of the passage that has been difficult?
- Is there a particular part of the plan that you've been reluctant to implement?
- What is the hardest part about memorization for you? What is the easiest part?

If the memorization thing is going great, yay! Take a few minutes to review Psalm 63, say the portion you know out loud a few times, and then check this box: ☐. Way to go! You're eating the scroll! *Hagah!*

If the memorization thing is not going well, don't despair! This is really normal. There is still hope for you and your spiritual taste buds. Just keep reading. We are going to try to breathe some new life into your plan.

REVITALIZE

There are lots of different methods for memorizing Scripture, but at the core of most of them is this concept: repetition over time. For someone like me who loves to check a box and consider something accomplished, repetition over time is a bit of an annoying concept. And yet? It's just about the only thing that will wedge the good stuff into my head. Here's a plan based on a memorization method by smart Bible person Andrew M. Davis[6] that will allow you to slowly but surely force-feed Psalm 63 into your brain. The best news? Your spiritual taste buds will begin to realize how very delicious it is to have God's Word hidden in your heart, and they'll be more likely to want to embrace the cost.

DAY 1

- Read verse 1 out loud ten times, trying to take a picture of the verse with your mind.
- Cover it up, and try to recite it ten times.

DAY 2

- Try to recite verse 1, ten times.
- Read verse 2 out loud ten times, trying to take a picture of the verse with your mind.
- Cover it up, and try to recite it ten times.

DAY 3

- Try to recite verses 1-2, ten times.
- Read verse 3 out loud ten times, trying to take a picture of the verse with your mind.
- Cover it up, and try to recite it ten times.

DAYS 4 AND ON

Keep pressing on in this pattern until all eleven verses in Psalm 63 are memorized. Once the whole thing is memorized, say the passage in its entirety every day for a month or two.

Here are some things you can do to ensure that you actually start taking these steps:

- Tell someone your plan and ask them to keep you accountable.
- Write each day's memorization task in your planner.
- Set an alarm to remind you of the task.
- Attach the memorization work to another habit, like brushing your teeth or your morning commute.
- Keep listening to those Psalm 63 songs we found!
- Collect verses that compare God's Word to honey and post them in places where you're likely to need encouragement.

CLOSING PRAYER

DEAR GOD,

You are my God. I want to earnestly seek You by hiding Your Word in my heart! I know You will satisfy my soul as my mouth praises You and as I meditate on You in the watches of the night. Strengthen me to store Your Words in my heart that I might truly understand that Your steadfast love is better than life.

AMEN.

CLOSING RHYTHM

Read Psalm 63 out loud, one last time. Hagah!

CONFIDENCE IN CHRIST

PSALM 63

1 *O God, you are my God; earnestly I seek you;*

my soul thirsts for you;

my flesh faints for you,

as in a dry and weary land where there is no water.

2 *So I have looked upon you in the sanctuary,*

beholding your power and glory.

3 *Because your steadfast love is better than life,*

my lips will praise you.

4 *So I will bless you as long as I live;*

in your name I will lift up my hands.

5 *My soul will be satisfied as with fat and rich food, and my mouth*

will praise you with joyful lips,

6 *when I remember you upon my bed,*

and meditate on you in the watches of the night;

7 *for you have been my help,*

and in the shadow of your wings I will sing for joy.

8 *My soul clings to you;*

your right hand upholds me.

9 *But those who seek to destroy my life*

shall go down into the depths of the earth;

10 *they shall be given over to the power of the sword;*

they shall be a portion for jackals.

11 *But the king shall rejoice in God;*

all who swear by him shall exult,

for the mouths of liars will be stopped.

WATCH & DISCUSS

Watch the video and make notes as we dig into verse 11 together. This week's video and discussion are all mixed together, so make sure you go back and discuss some of the questions and portions we skipped before moving on to the final evaluation.

In verse 11, we see David confident of two things.

1. _____   2. _____

C: CONTEXT

"THE KING"

Second Samuel 15:19 says, "Go back and stay with the king." In this verse, David is referring to _____.

READ 1 SAMUEL 16:6-13.

Who made David king? We don't have any way of knowing if David thought about this memory in the wilderness, but how might remembering this have contributed to David's confidence in verse 11?

"THE MOUTHS OF LIARS WILL BE STOPPED"

READ 2 SAMUEL 15:12; 15:30-31; 17:14.

Did David make an accurate proclamation that "the mouths of liars will be stopped"?

O: OBSERVATION

D: DEFINITIONS

Look up the following words first in an original language dictionary and then in an English dictionary if necessary.

"rejoice"

"exult"

"stopped"

Here's a fun fact: The Greek word for "stopped" is the same word used in Genesis 8:2 when God remembered Noah during the flood and He then closed the heavens and held back the rain.

Do you notice any delight packed into the meanings of "rejoice" and "exult"?

How does knowing the use of the word "stopped" in Genesis 8 enhance your understanding of "the mouths of liars will be stopped"?

T: THEMES
Theme bucket: Mouth

_____

_____

R: REPETITION
Draw arrows to indicate what is repeated.

I: INTERPRETATION
S: SCRIPTURE
READ PSALM 3.

Side note: One of the cross-references for Ps. 3:1 "how many are my foes!" is 2 Sam. 15:12 — the verse that tells us David's counselor Ahithophel has betrayed him to conspire with Absalom.

Hold it up against Psalm 63, particularly verse 11. How does Psalm 3 help you understand Psalm 63 a little better?

Why, according to Psalm 3, is David able to sleep? Why is he not afraid?

If you have time, look into some of the cross-references available for Psalm 63:11.

G: GOSPEL

The gospel is vivid in two different places. The first is when David calls himself the king, because he shows that his identity is secure. Christ followers can know that their identity is secure, too.

The second place I see the gospel is his confidence in the _____ of the _____.

C: CURIOSITY

Is there anything that piques your curiosity in this part of the passage? If there's time, chase it. If there's not time, plan to spend some of your Bible reading time this week chasing it.

A: APPLICATION

David is confident in his _____, and we can be confident in our _____, too.

The same hand that stops the mouths of liars and held back the rains during the worldwide flood in the time of Noah, is the hand that extends to us Living Water.

With your group, reflect on what Jesus said in John 4 to the woman at the well.

Are you hungry? Are you thirsty? Are you tired? Good—let that need drive you to the arms of your good Father, who has all that you need. Don't satisfy your cravings with lesser things. Earnestly seek after the Lord through His Word. Feast on it. Delight in it.

WHAT NOW?

Evaluate yourself after these eight weeks:

Do you feel better equipped to "earnestly seek" the Lord through Bible study?

How are you going to keep going in your pursuit to know and love God's Word? What's your next step?

Is His steadfast love better than life? We know the church answer is "yes," but let's realistically consider whether or not our hearts and souls believe it. If there is a disconnect from your head to your heart, what can you do? Perhaps this prayer from A.W. Tozer will help:

O God, I have tasted Thy goodness, and it has both satisfied me and made me thirsty for more. I am painfully conscious of my need of further grace. I am ashamed of my lack of desire. O God, the Triune God, I want to want Thee; I long to be filled with longing; I thirst to be made more thirsty still. Show me Thy glory, I pray Thee, that so I may know Thee indeed. Begin in mercy a new work of love within me. Say to my soul, 'Rise up, my love, my fair one, and come away.' Then give me grace to rise and follow Thee up from this misty lowland where I have wandered so long. In Jesus' Name, Amen.[1] **A.W. TOZER**

CLOSING PRAYER

DEAR GOD,

You are our God. Earnestly we seek You. Our soul thirsts for You; our flesh faints for You as in a dry and weary land where there is no water. We know that You offer Living Water and are the only one who can satisfy our thirst. We know Your steadfast love is better than life. We will rejoice in You because we know we are safe and we know You are the ultimate source of delight.

AMEN.

CLOSING RHYTHM

Read Psalm 63 out loud together. Remember, this Psalm was not just written for David's personal worship—it was purposefully included in the nation of Israel's songbook for the purpose of corporate worship. The original audience would have sung this out loud together!

LEADER GUIDE

PRAY DILIGENTLY. Ask God to prepare you to lead this study. Pray individually and specifically for the girls in your group. Make this a priority in your personal walk and preparation.

PREPARE ADEQUATELY. Don't just wing this. Take time to preview each session so you have a good grasp of the content. Look over the group session and consider your girls. Feel free to adjust the questions provided, and add other questions that fit your group better.

PROVIDE RESOURCES. Each student will need a Bible study book. Try to have extras on hand for girls who join the group later in the study. Also suggest girls bring a Bible and journal to group each week.

ENCOURAGE FREELY. Cheer for your girls and encourage them to participate in every part of the study.

LEAD BY EXAMPLE. Make sure you complete all of the personal study. Be willing to share your story, what you're learning, and your questions as you discuss together.

BE AWARE. If girls are hesitant to discuss their thoughts and questions in a larger group, consider dividing into smaller groups to provide a setting more conducive to conversation.

FOLLOW UP. If a student mentions a prayer request or need, make sure to follow up. It may be a situation where you can get others in the group involved in helping out.

EVALUATE OFTEN. After each session and throughout the study, assess what needs to be changed to more effectively lead the study.

1

GETTING STARTED: Kick off Session 1 by getting to know your girls and helping them get to know you. Our time together is going to be some serious study, so start out each group with some serious fun. Consider playing a game of "Find Your Match" or something similar as you begin. Allow the pairs to get to know each other a little better before coming back together.

WATCH: Encourage girls to follow along with the Session 1 video by using the fill-in-the-blank section, then discuss ideas or passages that stood out to you.

DISCUSS: In this first session, we're going to be discussing the why and helping girls evaluate where they are. Set a timer and give your girls the time and space to reflect as they journal about their relationship with God and His Word. You may want to play some music to fill any awkward silence. Be discerning about your group dynamic to determine whether they will be comfortable sharing their experiences or if they prefer keeping their answers private.

CLOSING: Go over the recipe one more time before you close. And then end your group time with the closing prayer and rhythm. The first couple of times this might feel a little weird, but the payoff is so going to be worth it.

GETTING STARTED: Let's play a game of "Shakespeare or the Bible." Beforehand, prepare a list of quotes and ask girls to guess whether they are from the Bible or Shakespeare. There are several lists readily available on the Internet to help you out. We'll quickly see in this game that context matters a lot and it's very easy to miss the point without the entire story.

WATCH: Encourage girls to follow along with the Session 2 video by using the fill-in-the-blank section. As you watch, you'll also want to begin filling in the context chart on page 28. Encourage girls to continue coming back to this page during your discussion and as you complete the personal study days.

DISCUSS: Today we're going to be doing a lot of digging into the recipe. Make sure girls are following along and understand the recipe in order to keep going on their own at home. It might also be helpful to have a selection of different colored pens and highlighters for girls to mark up their Context Chart and Scripture page.

CLOSING: End your group time with the closing prayer and rhythm. The first couple of times this might feel a little weird, but the payoff is so going to be worth it.

3

GETTING STARTED: This week is all about relationships. Okay, it's not, but we are going to DTR. So let's start with a Best Friends edition of the Newlywed Game. Select two girls to be tested and ask them write down the answers to questions about each other. Make sure these are lighthearted and appropriate for your group. After each question, ask the girls to reveal their answers to see if they got them correct.

WATCH: Before you start the video, go over your context chart together and add anything you may have missed in your personal study days. Watch the video and encourage girls to follow along by using the fill-in-the-blank section, then discuss ideas or passages that stood out to you.

DISCUSS: This week we're going to be closely looking at the words of Psalm 63. Make sure you are familiar with some of the definition tools in order to help girls and prevent future frustration, and refer to the references in the back of the book for help. Girls will continue using the rest of the recipe in their personal study, so make sure they are comfortable using the DTR tools before closing.

CLOSING: End your group time with the closing prayer and rhythm. The first couple of times this might feel a little weird, but the payoff is so going to be worth it.

4

GETTING STARTED: I love ice cream. You love ice cream. It's a fact, so let's start with an ice cream game. Ask each girl to write down her favorite ice cream flavor on a piece of paper and place it in a bowl. Then the first volunteer is going to try to match a flavor with each girl. If she gets it wrong, it moves on to the next girl. Keep going until you know everyone's favorite ice cream flavor. (Maybe keep this info locked in your head for a fun surprise later on.)

WATCH: Encourage girls to follow along with the Session 4 video by using the fill-in-the-blank section, then discuss ideas or passages that stood out to you.

DISCUSS: This week we are going to focus on interpretation. It's something we do every day without even thinking. As you get started, ask the girls to consider how they interpret different writing styles. How is a billboard different from a text from your crush? The Bible can seem confusing and quitting may be easier than trying, but God's Word is full of delight when we know what steps to follow next. Continue encouraging girls to mark up the Scripture pages at the beginning of each session as we dig further into Psalm 63.

CLOSING: Now you're really getting the hang of this. End your group time with the closing prayer and rhythm. Is it coming easier to you now?

5

GETTING STARTED: This week's video is a little longer and is going to take some more time and concentration to make it through. So let's keep this quick today and have a rock, paper, scissors tournament. Consider having a small prize for the champion like a gift card, new scrunchie, or a bag of candy.

WATCH: Encourage girls to follow along with the Session 5 video by filling in Scripture references and notes for each movement of The Story of Hunger. Since today's video is longer than most, you may need to take a break in the middle for a quick snack or brain break. After watching the video, discuss ideas or passages that stood out to you.

DISCUSS: The Story of Hunger is a way to tell the story of Jesus and the gospel as one big story. This may be a new idea to many students so spend as much time as you need looking at the Bible as one story and discussing how that idea is present and can be seen in Psalm 63. Looking ahead, Day 3-4 is one long personal day, so prepare girls to spend some extra time on Day 3 or break it up into two days.

CLOSING: End your group time with the closing prayer and rhythm. Play a song from the Psalm 63 list as you pray together.

6

GETTING STARTED: Let's start this week with a drawing contest. The middle of the night can be a scary time for anybody, so challenge your girls to draw a picture of what scares them or what gives them comfort. Before you watch the video, discuss what a few of those scary things are for your girls and ask how they cope. This doesn't have to be a spiritual answer—Instagram or Tik Tok might be the honest answer for you and several of your teens.

WATCH: Encourage girls to follow along with the Session 6 video by using the fill-in-the-blank section, then discuss ideas or passages that stood out to you.

DISCUSS: This week we're really going to be looking at David's life while writing this Psalm. He is filled with peace and assurance while in a literal desert and running for his life. Ask girls to consider if they have ever experienced a time of ongoing fear or loneliness in the middle of the night. Compare your experiences to David's in verses 5-8. This session's group time is a little shorter than most, so you may want to look ahead to Day 4. We are going to make a memorization plan and it could help girls prepare for the week to start thinking about it now. You may even want to offer some kind of incentive for those who memorize it!

CLOSING: End your group time with the closing prayer and rhythm. Check in with girls during the week to make sure they are working on their memorization plan and are ready to share it next week.

7

GETTING STARTED: Before you begin the video, ask the girls to present their memorization plans and make sure they are all on track. Ask if anyone is ready to recite the entire Psalm from memory. They may surprise themselves at how well they already know it.

WATCH: Encourage girls to follow along with the Session 7 video by using the fill-in-the-blank section and continuing with the Theme Buckets. We will be going deeper into observation and you have the opportunity to work through the passage with me or you can study the themes on your own.

DISCUSS: This week we are going to take a deep dive into observation by studying the themes found in Psalm 63. Fill in the themes as you watch the video and be sure to discuss your observations together after. One of those may be, "Body parts? Gross!" Continue discussing and comparing the themes as you answer the final discussion questions.

CLOSING: End your group time with the closing prayer and rhythm. Students are really going to be studying the text this week, so be sure they are staying motivated and keeping up with their personal study days.

8

GETTING STARTED: There is some weird stuff in the Bible that we don't usually spend time going over in our Bible study groups. Choose a few of those stories from the Bible (such as Balaam's talking donkey and Lot's wife being turned into a pillar of salt), and write them on slips of paper for girls to choose from and then play a game of Pictionary. Divide into two teams so girls can take turns drawing and guessing what the other group has drawn.

WATCH: Encourage girls to follow along with the Session 8 video by using the fill-in-the-blank section, then discuss ideas or passages that stood out to you.

DISCUSS: When we don't understand something in the Bible or it just sounds too strange, we just skip over it, right? But we aren't going to do that anymore because we are going to use our recipe to understand the weird stuff in the Bible. This week, we're going to use interpretation and SGC to dig into verses 9-10. Before group time, remind girls to have their Bible with them or a Bible app on their phone because we're going to be looking at several different verses as we study the text.

CLOSING: End your group time with the closing prayer and rhythm. We just have one more week left and the final verse! Encourage your girls to finish strong and complete the final days of personal study.

9

GETTING STARTED: You did it! You made it to the end. You deserve to be celebrated and so do your girls! Plan something special for them this week—cupcakes, confetti, or maybe those ice cream flavors we talked about. Before we get going, allow your girls the chance to recite Psalm 63 from memory. Feel free to throw some confetti as each girl completes the psalm. It is truly something to be celebrated that your girls have stored God's Word in their hearts.

WATCH: Make notes as we dig into verse 11 together in the video. Make sure to go back and discuss some of the questions and portions we skipped before moving on.

DISCUSS: This final session is going to be a little different. We are going to work through the entire COIA recipe together looking at verse 11. Fill in the blanks as you watch the video and take notes on anything that stands out. Be sure to discuss the portions we don't cover in the video before moving on to the final discussion questions.

CLOSING: Just because this Bible study has come to a close does not mean you should stop using the COIA Method to study the Bible. My hope is that you can now apply the tools you have learned over the last nine weeks to any passage of Scripture. Keep connecting with your girls and studying the Bible. Ask them how they would like to connect and stay accountable in studying God's Word.

SOURCES

SESSION 1

1. Jen Wilkin, *Women of the Word: How to Study the Bible with Both Our Hearts and Our Minds* (Wheaton: Crossway, 2019), 64.

2. "fold." Merriam-Webster.com. Accessed Jan. 10, 2020, https://www.merriam-webster.com.

SESSION 2

1. causing or characterized by severe pain, suffering, or sorrow; "grievous." Merriam-Webster.com. Accessed Jan. 10, 2020, https://www.merriam-webster.com.

2. Mel Lawrenz, The Many Gneres of Scripture. Accessed Jan. 10, 2020. https://www.biblegateway.com/blog/2016/03/the-many-genres-of-scripture.

3. Dr. James Strong, BlueLetterBible.com; Strong, James. Strong's Definitions. Blue Letter Bible. 1890. Accessed Jan. 10, 2020, https://www.blueletterbible.org/lang/lexicon/lexicon.cfm?Strongs=H7836&t=CSB.

4. "diligent." Merriam-Webster.com. Accessed Jan. 10, 2020, https://www.merriam-webster.com.

5. Site: http://www.jesuswalk.com/david/life_of_david_maps_and_graphics.htm Map: http://www.jesuswalk.com/david/maps/rebellion-of-absalom-map-2sam-15-19-1200x1748x300.jpg.

6. Dr. James Strong, BlueLetterBible.com; Strong, James. Strong's Definitions. Blue Letter Bible. 1890. Accessed Jan. 10, 2020, https://www.blueletterbible.org/lang/lexicon/lexicon.cfm?Strongs=H5889&t=ESV.

SESSION 3

1. John J. Medina, *Brain Rules: 12 Principles for Surviving and Thriving at Work, Home, and School.* (Seattle: Pear Press, 2014), 93.

2. "What's an Interlinear Bible? - Inside BST." Bible Study Tools. Accessed Nov. 10, 2019. https://www.biblestudytools.com/blogs/inside-bst/what-s-an-interlinear-bible.html.

3. Dr. James Strong, BlueLetterBible.com; Strong, James. Strong's Definitions. Blue Letter Bible. 1890. Accessed Nov. 20, 2019, https://www.blueletterbible.org/lang/lexicon/lexicon.cfm?Strongs=H2372&t=ESV.

4. *The Emperor's New Groove (2000).* IMDB. Directed by Mark Dindal. Accessed Jan. 10, 2020. https://www.imdb.com/title/tt0120917/characters/nm0911320.

5. Dr. James Strong, BlueLetterBible.com; Strong, James. Strong's Definitions. Blue Letter Bible. 1890. Accessed Nov. 20, 2019, https://www.blueletterbible.org/lang/lexicon/lexicon.cfm?Strongs=H3651&t=ESV.

6. Eugene H. Merrill, "Psalm 63: Finding Satisfaction in God," in *Interpreting the Psalms for Teaching and Preaching*, ed. by Herbert W. Bateman IV and D. Brent Sandy (St. Louis: Chalice Press, 2010), 88-89.

7. Dr. James Strong, BlueLetterBible.com; Strong, James. Strong's Definitions. Blue Letter Bible. 1890. Accessed Nov. 20, 2019, https://www.blueletterbible.org/lang/lexicon/lexicon.cfm?Strongs=H6944&t=ESV.

8. "sanctuary." Merriam-Webster.com. Accessed Nov. 20, 2019, https://www.merriam-webster.com.

9. "sacred." Merriam-Webster.com. Accessed Nov. 20, 2019. https://www.merriam-webster.com.

SESSION 4

1. *ESV Gospel Transformation Study Bible* (Wheaton, IL: Crossway, 2019), 787.

2. Dr. James Strong, BlueLetterBible.com; Strong, James. Strong's Definitions. Blue Letter Bible. 1890. Accessed Jan. 18, 2020, https://www.blueletterbible.org/lang/lexicon/lexicon.cfm?Strongs=H2416&t=ESV.

3. Keller, Timothy. "The Discipline of Desire II." Sermon, Redeemer Presbyterian Church, New York, NY, January 26, 1997.

4. Ibid.

5. TagalogLang. "GIGIL: English Translation, Explanation of the Filipino Word." Tagalong Lang, August 31, 2019. https://www.tagaloglang.com/gigil.

6. Irving L. Jensen, *Enjoy Your Bible: Making the Most of Your Time with God's Word*, (World Wide Publications, 1969), 96.

7. John Piper. "What Is Worship?" Desiring God, Accessed Jan. 18, 2020, https://www.desiringgod.org/interviews/what-is-worship.

SESSION 5

1. Metanarrative movements adapted from https://thebibleproject.com/podcast/what-story-bible.

2. "Psalm 63." ESV Bible. Crossway, 2020. https://www.esv.org/Psalm 63.

3. Tim Keller's sermon "Discipline of Desire II" helped to shape this line of thinking: Keller, Timothy. "The Discipline of Desire II." Sermon, Redeemer Presbyterian Church, New York, NY, January 26, 1997.

4. Eugene H. Peterson, *Praying with the Psalms: A Year of Daily Prayers and Reflections on the Words of David*. (San Francisco, CA: Harper San Francisco, 1993), May 4.

SESSION 6

1. Tim Mackie and Jon Collins. "How to Read the Bible, Part 6: Jewish Scripture Meditation Vs Modern Meditation". The Bible Project. Podcast audio, August 11, 2017. https://thebibleproject.com/podcast/how-read-bible-part-6-jewish-scripture-meditation-vs-modern-meditation.

2. Kevin D. Mahoney, "Latin Definition for: Studium, Studi(i)," Latdict, accessed January 31, 2020, https://latin-dictionary.net/definition/35840/studium-studi-i).

3. "zeal."Merriam-Webster.com. Accessed Jan. 31, 2020, https://www.merriam-webster.com.

4. Timothy Keller, *The Songs of Jesus: A Year of Daily Devotions in the Psalms* (New York: Viking, 2015), 135.

5. Tim Mackie and Jon Collins. "How to Read the Bible, Part 6: Jewish Scripture Meditation Vs Modern Meditation". The Bible Project. Podcast audio, August 11, 2017. https://thebibleproject.com/podcast/how-read-bible-part-6-jewish-scripture-meditation-vs-modern-meditation/.

6. John J. Medina, *Brain Rules: 12 Principles for Surviving and Thriving at Work, Home, and School*. (Seattle: Pear Press, 2014), 133.

7. John J. Medina, *Brain Rules: 12 Principles for Surviving and Thriving at Work, Home, and School*. (Seattle: Pear Press, 2014), 131.

SESSION 7

1. *ESV Gospel Transformation Study Bible* (Wheaton, IL: Crossway, 2019), 787.

2. Nancy Guthrie, *The Wisdom of God: Seeing Jesus in the Psalms & Wisdom Books* (Wheaton, IL: Crossway, 2012), 71.

SESSION 8

1. Brian Malcolm, "Of Christ the Mediator," The 1689 Baptist Confession of Faith, May 25, 2017, https://www.the1689confession.com/chapter-8.

2. "curiosity."Merriam-Webster.com. Accessed Feb. 10, 2020, https://www.merriam-webster.com.

3. Nat Geo WILD, YouTube (YouTube, September 20, 2016), https://www.youtube.com/watch?v=AhEdKY4ujjg.

4. "Anubis," Anubis - Explore Deities of Ancient Egypt, accessed Feb. 12, 2020, https://egyptianmuseum.org/deities-Anubis.

5. Jackals (20 Occurrences). Accessed Feb. 12, 2020, https://bibleapps.com/j/jackals.htm.

6. Andrew M. Davis, *An Approach to Extended Memorization of Scripture* (Greenville, SC: Ambassador International, 2014).

SESSION 9

1. A. W. Tozer, *The Pursuit of God* (Camp Hill, PA: Christian Publishing, Inc., 1982), 20.

PSALM 63 SONGS

As any girl with a song stuck in her head can attest, humans have a unique ability to absorb songs. Originally, the Psalms were designed to be sung out loud as a part of corporate worship. When you sing Psalm 63 (or any psalm), you are joining in a long, rich heritage of worshipers singing praise to God, and your soul is benefiting from God's good design for our souls to easily and delightedly slurp up songs like a delicious milkshake.

You can find my full Psalm 63 playlist on Spotify, or search for each song individually using the list below. Though many of these songs feature different translations of Psalm 63 than the ESV translation we're diving into in this study, all of these songs will help you understand the text better, hide Psalm 63 in your heart long-term, and lead you in worshiping the Lord through His Word!

- Psalm 63 (Better Than Life) by Shane & Shane

- Psalm 63 (Better Than Life) [feat. Lindsey Kidd] by Robbie Seay Band

This one is my favorite!

- Psalm 63 (Steadfast Love) by New Hope Oahu

- O God You Are My God (Psalm 63) by Scott Brenner

- Psalm 63 (Better Than Life) [feat. Jeremy Moore] by Advent Birmingham

- Psalm 63 (O God You Are My God) [Live] by NLC (New Life Church)

- Oh God, You Are My God (Psalm 63) by Fernando Ortega

- Psalm 63 by The Corner Room

- As Long As I Live (Psalm 63) by The Sing Team

ANATOMY OF AN ORIGINAL LANGUAGE DEFINITION

Strong's Concordance is basically a gigantic index of the words in the Bible. It was published in 1890, and has long been a "go-to" resource (and thanks to the internet, an accessible resource!) for Bible study.

The **transliteration** of the word, which is a representation of the word in another language. Basically, this is the best shot at representing this Hebrew word in an "English-y" way. Another transliteration is "hesed," which is what we use in this study!

Pronunciation (just like in an English dictionary)

Strong's Definitions

חֶסֶד checed *(kheh'-sed)* from H2616; kindness; by implication (towards God) piety; rarely (by opposition) reproof, or (subjectively) beauty:—favour, good deed(-liness, -ness), kindly, (loving-) kindness, merciful (kindness), mercy, pity, reproach, wicked thing.

The **root word** written in its original language (typically Hebrew in the Old Testament or Greek in the New Testament).

In Strong's Concordance, each original language word has a **corresponding number**. This helps a Bible student determine the Hebrew or Greek word and see other verses in the Bible where that word is used.

The **definition**. Just like with an English dictionary, let the context help you determine which meaning is most appropriate. Don't just pick the one you like! If you need help, pray for wisdom (Jas. 1:5, Ps. 119:18), and ask another Bible student to help you.

BIBLE TRANSLATIONS

There are lots of different Bible translations out there, so it can be confusing to know what to read. All of the different translations are valuable because they help us know God better, but I recommend primarily using a readable word-for-word translation or a respected word-for-word and thought-for-thought blend for Bible study because these translations stick to the Hebrew and Greek wording as closely as they can. However, having a secondary thought-for-thought translation can help when you get stuck. These translations take the original thoughts and seek to clearly communicate them in a way readers can best understand. Finally, there are paraphrase translations, which are super easy to read and can help enhance your understanding of a passage, but they are probably not the best for in-depth study. Paraphrases are a great option when you need a reprieve from deep study and desire to simply read.

WORD-FOR-WORD TRANSLATIONS	WORD-FOR-WORD & THOUGHT-FOR-THOUGHT BLENDS
English Standard Version (ESV)	New International Version (NIV)
New American Standard Bible (NASB)	Christian Standard Bible (CSB)

THOUGHT-FOR-THOUGHT TRANSLATIONS	PARAPHRASE
New Living Translation (NLT)	The Message (MSG)

This is what I use, and what we're using in this study!

LIST OF GENRES

Did you know the Bible contains all kinds of different genres? Genre is important because it impacts the way we process words. For example, you wouldn't process a recipe the same way you would song lyrics. They are completely different categories of writing! (It won't do you much good to sing a recipe or make cookies by following song lyrics.) When you study a book of the Bible, take the time to carefully consider its genre, using the list below to help you.

- **HISTORICAL NARRATIVE:** "Narrative" means it tells a story, and you can find plenty of narration in books like Genesis, Nehemiah, and 1 and 2 Samuel. The "historical" part of this category is important, because it reminds us these are actual events, not merely Sunday school stories. When you read historical narrative, pay attention to the common elements of story you probably learned about in English class, like characters, setting, conflict, climax, resolution, and the impact the ending has on future stories. Often these narratives aren't tidy, because real life isn't tidy!

- **LAW:** You'll know a book or passage, like Deuteronomy, falls into this category if it lists commands. These commands are designed to give life-giving boundaries to prevent God's people from stepping into things that are dishonoring to God and are bad for them and others. Often, law passages can be found tucked into historical narratives.

- **WISDOM:** In Wisdom books, such as Proverbs and Ecclesiastes, the writers give direction for practical ways to live in a way that honors God and grows good fruit. This helpful instruction reveals general ways a person can live wisely.

- **POETRY:** Poems in the Bible (like those in Song of Solomon, the Psalms, and even tucked into historical narrative and letters) were written to point us to God through creative, image-rich language. You'll often find poets borrowing from their other senses (like touch and taste) to describe what God is doing in their souls. These are not intended to be read like an instruction manual but experienced like art. Even within poetry, like the Psalms, there are some sub-genres. Because the Psalms are poems originally intended to be sung, they can fall into many different categories. Some sub-genres include lament (crying out in pain), hymns (worship), imprecations (curses), wisdom, history, and thanksgiving.

• **PROPHECY:** A prophet (like Amos and Jeremiah) is one who speaks on God's behalf and reveals things to come. God spoke to His people through many prophets, and these words reveal important things about God—what grieves Him, what His plans are, what He desires for His people. As you read prophecy books, take special care to investigate the specific time and place to which God is speaking through His prophet.

• **GOSPELS:** The Gospels (Matthew, Mark, Luke, and John) are retellings of Jesus' life on earth. They are historical narrative, but they are a special kind of historical narrative because they are a stunning proclamation of good news (that's what the word "gospel" means) for all people.

• **LETTERS:** After everything that happened in the Gospels shook the world, church leaders like Paul, under the inspiration of the Holy Spirit, wrote letters to help Jesus' followers understand how the gospel message impacts their daily lives. You'll know a book falls into this category typically because it begins with the writer greeting his audience. Read letters like you would an actual letter—reading the whole thing in one sitting and then taking time to process the various pieces with the full text in mind. Wouldn't it be weird to pick up a letter someone sent you and deep-dive into the third section without reading the others? That's why, if you want to read James' letter, you should be sure to read the whole thing.

• **APOCALYPTIC:** Apocalyptic books like Revelation and Daniel are similar to prophecy books, because they are God's way of giving a peek into His future plans, especially in regard to Jesus' second coming. Though these books often seem mysterious, they are an encouraging reminder that God is at work, even when we don't understand everything He's doing.